A publication in
The Adult Education Association
Handbook Series in Adult Education

Changing
Approaches
to Studying
Adult Education

*Huey B. Long
Roger Hiemstra
and Associates*

Changing
Approaches
to Studying
Adult Education

Jossey-Bass Publishers
San Francisco • Washington • London • 1980

CHANGING APPROACHES TO STUDYING ADULT EDUCATION
by Huey B. Long, Roger Hiemstra, and Associates

Copyright © 1980 by: Adult Education Association
of the United States of America
810 Eighteenth Street, N.W.
Washington, D.C. 20006

Jossey-Bass Inc., Publishers
433 California Street
San Francisco, California 94104

Jossey-Bass Limited
28 Banner Street
London EC1Y 8QE

Library of Congress Cataloging in Publication Data

Long, Huey B
    Changing approaches to studying adult education.

    (Adult Education Association handbook series in
adult education)
    Bibliography: p. 138
    Includes index.
    1. Adult education—Research—Addresses, essays,
lectures. I. Hiemstra, Roger, joint author.
II. Title. III. Series: Adult Education Association.
Adult Education Association handbook series in adult
education.
LC5219.L583   374   78-62579
ISBN 0-87589-447-X

Manufactured in the United States of America

JACKET DESIGN BY WILLI BAUM

FIRST EDITION

Code 8008

The AEA Handbook Series in Adult Education

WILLIAM S. GRIFFITH
University of British Columbia

HOWARD Y. MCCLUSKY
University of Michigan

General Editors

Edgar J. Boone,
Ronald W. Shearon,
Estelle E. White,
and Associates
Serving Personal and
Community Needs Through
Adult Education
April 1980

John M. Peters
and Associates
Building and Effective
Adult Education
Enterprise
April 1980

Huey B. Long
Roger Hiemstra
and Associates
Changing Approaches
to Studying Adult
Education
April 1980

Foreword

Adult education as a field of study and of practice is not well understood by many literate and intelligent American adults whose exposure to the field has been limited to one or a few aspects of its apparently bewildering mosaic. Since 1926, when the American Association for Adult Education (AAAE) was founded, the leaders of that organization and its successor, the Adult Education Association of the U.S.A. (AEA), have striven to communicate both to the neophytes in the field and to the adult public an understanding of its diverse and complex enterprises. A major vehicle for accomplishing this communication has been a sequence of handbooks of adult education, issued periodically to convey a broad view of the mosaic. In 1934, 1936, and 1948 the AAAE published the first three handbooks. Although the Association had intended to issue a handbook every two years, that plan was not carried out for a number of reasons, including the outbreak of World War II and the termination of support by the Carnegie Corporation. Within three years of the publication of the 1948 handbook the Association itself dissolved in order to establish the AEA, which included the former members of both the AAAE and the Department of Adult Education of the National Education Association. It was nine years before the AEA was able to publish its first handbook, the fourth in the sequence, followed a decade later by the fifth version.

In the early 1970s both the Publications Committee of AEA and the Commission of the Professors of Adult Education (an

affiliated organization of the AEA) explored the kinds of handbooks
that could be designed to serve the changing nature and needs of
the field. They found that different parts of the field were developing at different rates—in some areas information was becoming
outdated rapidly, whereas in others a decennial handbook would be
adequate to maintain currency. Moreover, the growing literature
and the many developments in policies and programs led them to
conclude that a single volume of traditional size would not be sufficient to treat the expanding knowledge base, the changing policies
and practices, and the controversial topics in adult education.
Accordingly, the Publications Committee decided that the next
handbook would consist of several volumes, allowing the presentation of an increased amount of information on each of nine selected
parts of the field and preparing the way for subsequent revisions of
each volume independently on a schedule reflecting the pace of
change in each area. The result is The AEA Handbook Series in
Adult Education, which is being developed by the general editors
with the guidance and assistance of the Publications Committee.

The present book, *Changing Approaches to Studying Adult
Education,* was originally prepared at the request of the Commission
of the Professors of Adult Education. But during its development
the Publications Committee concluded that it should be a volume
in the Handbook Series. The other eight volumes were conceived
after extensive consultation between the general editors and the
Publications Committee. These books deal with building effective
adult education enterprises, serving community needs, administering
adult education, redefining the discipline, responsibilities of adult
education, comparative adult education, training, and instruction.

Preparation of the series required the cooperation and dedi-
cated efforts of scores of chapter authors, Publication Committee
chairmen and members, and successive executive committees of the
AEA. In bringing together the insights and perceptions of adult
education scholars, the series is a major contribution of the Association to the advancement of an understanding of adult education as
a field of study and of practice.

January 1980   WILLIAM S. GRIFFITH
                                                        HOWARD Y. MCCLUSKY
                                                        General Editors

Preface

Etymologically the word *adult* is derived from the Latin verb *adoles-cere,* meaning to come to maturity, and is a form of the past participle *adultus;* it denotes that which has matured, is no longer growing and developing. Thus the root of the word suggests why scholars and others were for years content to define adulthood merely as the stage between adolescence and old age, as a time of no change between periods of growth and decline. Indeed, for the past half century educators of adults have often believed that very few others were interested in the adult, since too frequently people have believed that the adult has already acquired all the knowledge and habits he is going to have. People have therefore been reluctant to explore that mysterious "black box" known as adulthood.

Recently, however, a dramatic reversal has occurred. Suddenly adult educators are not alone in considering adulthood the most significant, as well as the longest, stage of life. An important reason for this change is the demographic shift in the American population: soon the majority of this country's citizens will be thirty years of age or older. Whatever the other causes—and we will not go into them here—it is true that in an increasing number of professional and occupational fields, interest in the adult has become almost a fascination; it is as if science had discovered a new human species. And study of the new species is attracting people from a wide spectrum, in medicine, the social services, in government, foundations, and education. Although the authors of this book frequently use the term *adult education* to refer to a specific field of research interest, the book is not limited to adult educators or to adult education. We believe that students and professionals from a variety of occupations can benefit from what we as adult educators have learned about the study of adults in the past fifty years.

This book, then, is about the study of adults primarily as conducted and perceived by some adult educators. As is pointed out in Chapter One, research has been a continuing topic of interest among adult educators. But heretofore, adult education research has been discussed in a variety of unrelated publications, an article here and one there, appearing over a period of years. Thus this publication is different in that it contains a number of chapters written by a variety of authors at about the same time. It may represent an evolutionary step in the study of the adult.

As the only handbook devoted exclusively to research in the present series, it must treat a wide range of topics from fairly general to rather specific. Two of our objectives were to provide constructive comment on the status of research in the field and to contribute to an improved conception of adult education by creating a better understanding of some of the more popular research methods employed by adult educators, as well as some appropriate methods that perhaps should be used more extensively. We chose the general review as the best means of achieving those goals. The book, thus, was not planned to provide an in-depth treatment of research methodology, designs, statistics, and similar topics. And, of necessity, it reflects the uneven use of different research methods among the hundreds of investigations annually conducted by adult educators and other researchers in various related fields. Neither was the book designed to interpret the variety of adult education research by topic and results, as did Brunner and others' classic work (1959). But even though we do not attempt to provide answers to specific methodological questions, general guidelines to correct some common, frequent, and customary errors are provided throughout. The emphasis is on the practice and philosophy of adult education research and what may be considered its distinctive aspects. Supporting illustrations and examples from adult research are provided whenever appropriate.

Occasional overlaps among authors were permitted because of the significance of the topics discussed and the nature of each author's assignment. While there is a certain risk in the pluralistic discussion of selected topics, we determined that restricted and controlled duplication was preferable to requiring the reader to move back and forth among the chapters frequently or to depend heavily on recall.

The nine chapters take up the major areas of interest in the conduct of research on adult subjects. Four chapters examine specific research methods: the two on survey research and grounded theory reflect the prevalence of descriptive research; the other two discuss experimental research and historical research. The following definitions of research methods used by DeCrow (1967), Grabowski (1973), and Grabowski and Loague (1970) are employed in this publication.

1. Experimental research is based on a design that is primarily used to test hypotheses concerned with cause and effect, or a design that includes control groups, randomization procedures, and manipulation of independent variables to control pertinent factors as much as possible. Such variables are quantitatively described.
2. Descriptive research is based on designs that require survey and descriptive activity to establish the status of the selected phenomenon or to assess the characteristics of a population. Such activity usually focuses on people, vital facts about their beliefs, opinions, attitudes, motivations, and behavior.
3. Historical research is based on critical investigation of events, developments, and experiences of the past, the careful weighing of evidence of the validity of information sources, and the interpretation of the evidence.

Each chapter analyzes and discusses the application of a particular research method, compares the use of selected methods within adult education, or examines trends and problems in the selection and use of various methods by specific groups.

In Chapter One Huey B. Long provides a brief look at some of the incentives for conducting research concerning adult phenomena. Long suggests that the expansion and elaboration of programs designed to serve adults has helped to focus attention and interest on adult research questions. He then presents a working definition of adult education research before reviewing what has been written about it. Three kinds of literature are explicated: literature that deals with the role of research in academic programs, bibliographic literature, and, most important, the descriptive and analytical literature.

Chapter Two has a more practical task: to assist the novice researcher with planning, practicing, and reporting research. Huey B. Long and Roger Hiemstra describe how to organize and pursue a research question for a thesis or dissertation. Some common characteristics in the practice of research in graduate programs are also discussed. These commonalities include the needs of the adult educator as they relate to research, the needs of the field as they are addressed by graduate research, the approach to research, and the preparation of a research proposal and a dissertation.

Robert A. Carlson, in the third chapter, says that a philosophical or humanistic history will challenge assumptions upon which the profession is based, and because of its potential for challenging basic assumptions, this type of research may offer a unique opportunity to those involved in the study of adult education. Writers of humanistic historical research are reminded that they have concomitant responsibilities for careful investigation and for high-quality literary scholarship. The literary scholarship and thesis development are best accomplished, according to Carlson, through a "playwright historian" concept whereby the writer rings up the curtain on the time he chooses, selects the lead characters and bit players, and develops the plot by selection and arrangement of the facts.

Chapter Four, by Gary Dickinson and Adrian Blunt, describes the role of the survey method, identifies its strengths and weaknesses, and discusses the flow of activities, together with the problems typically encountered in planning and conducting surveys. Since 1851 the survey has been employed to study a variety of topics, including personnel and staffing, adults' learning needs and interests, program activities, finance, and participation. And the authors believe the survey will probably continue to be the chosen method in most studies of adult education.

"Field Research and Grounded Theory" by Gordon G. Darkenwald is basic and practical, as it is addressed primarily to researchers who may be interested in, but unfamiliar with, grounded theory. Darkenwald believes grounded-theory research is probably more difficult than the typical descriptive or experimental study. The difficulty arises from several sources, including the absence of easily understood, codified rules for the collection and analysis of data and the construction of theory. Darkenwald gives several examples of both successful and unsuccessful applications of grounded theory in adult education.

In Chapter Six, Huey B. Long discusses several topics pertaining to experimental research: basic logic, hypotheses, designs, the handling of critical elements of the experimental design in adult education research, and the reasons why experimental research is not done more often and why it should be. Long suggests that an understanding of basic logic and Mill's canons should be helpful to the individual designing an experimental research project. He also predicts that the experimental method will be used more frequently as the fund of knowledge derived from descriptive research expands; the experimental method will be required to test explanations for important phenomena in the field.

Robert D. Boyd then tackles the following aspects of methodology: conjecture and its relation to the theoretical framework, to falsifiability, and to null hypotheses; the connection between concepts and method; reliability and validity; objectivety and intersubjectivity; categorization; and instrument development and testing. Boyd points out several common errors found in adult education research, such as the mismatching of methods and hypotheses and the failure to understand how concepts are inescapably imbedded in a theoretical framework.

In Chapter Eight Stanley M. Grabowski presents trends in graduate research since 1935. The data for his analysis were provided by the former ERIC Clearinghouse on Adult Education at Syracuse University. He looks at the quantity and quality of research, the topics studied, and the methods used. To support his conclusions concerning the trend toward higher quality, he cites several analyses of portions of the adult education literature. He also cites improvements in research design that strengthen internal and external validity and an improved theoretical structure as elements that contribute to the qualitative improvements.

Past, present, and future aspects of investigation into the education of adults are discussed by Hiemstra and Long in the Epilogue. In this brief chapter they summarize the research heritage, discuss emerging theories, and make some observations concerning future directions. As they see it, the expected changes in adult education research will not be radical. They predict that the field will benefit from the research activity of specialists in other areas, such as biology, chemistry, computer science, gerontology, and physiology. In addition, a kind of detente between the quantitatively oriented and qualitatively oriented researchers may be reached. Increased use of intensive experimental designs and path-analysis techniques is also noted as a possibility. The Epilogue is admittedly optimistic about the future results of adult education research.

February 1980   Huey B. Long
                                                      Atlanta, Georgia

                                                      Roger Hiemstra
                                                         Ames, Iowa

Contents

The Authors

ADRIAN BLUNT, doctoral student, Department of Adult Education, University of British Columbia

ROBERT D. BOYD, professor of Adult Education, University of Wisconsin–Madison

ROBERT A. CARLSON, professor of Adult Education, University of Saskatchewan

GORDON G. DARKENWALD, associate professor of Adult Education, Teachers College, Columbia University

GARY DICKINSON, associate professor of Adult Education, University of British Columbia

STANLEY M. GRABOWSKI, professor of Adult Education, Boston University

ROGER HIEMSTRA, professor of Adult Education, Iowa State University

HUEY B. LONG, professor of Adult Education, University of Georgia

Changing
Approaches
to Studying
Adult Education

Chapter One

A Perspective
on Adult Education
Research

Huey B. Long

One's perception of a phenomenon is determined in part by the angle and distance at which the phenomenon is viewed. Because perspective has such an important effect on one's mental images of phenomena, this chapter is designed to help readers establish a common position from which they can view adult education research. Accordingly, it has a fourfold mission: to look briefly at research incentives in adult education, to define adult education research, to discuss its special characteristics, and to review the relevant literature.

Research Incentives

Several elements are interacting to generate incentives for inquiry into adulthood and all of its social, psychological, economic, and political significance. These elements include our limited knowledge of adulthood; the peculiarities of adulthood, which suggest that a subtle distinctiveness characterizes research on this subject; and the rapid expansion of programs designed specifically for adults.

Formerly, adults were often viewed in an undifferentiated manner. Too little thought was given to how they differed from one another or from children. And even with the phenomenal increase in research concerning the human life cycle, we still know little about the life stages; our knowledge of the transitions from adolescence to middle age to senescence remains embarrassingly limited. We are also insufficiently informed about how the concepts of adult learning and continuing education have changed, as well as about the changing cultural influences on adult behavior. We are even short on information concerning how behavior is culturally conditioned. Because of the significance of adulthood and the extent of our ignorance of important life roles having to do with leisure, family life, and work, substantial research is needed.

However, in seeking to answer questions about adulthood, we cannot just shift labor and research instruments from a child population to an adult population. The ways in which adults differ from children, the conditions under which the study of adults is usually conducted, and the character of the field in which the researcher is working (adult education as opposed to psychology, for instance) all make research on adulthood subtly unique. For one thing, researchers concerned with adult behavior—more than researchers dealing with childhood—frequently have some kind of relationship with the individuals from whom data are collected. In addition, the questions investigated in adult education and related human resource development fields are usually embedded in a complex content. And the variables one wants to examine are often particularly difficult to isolate and to observe in adult research. Yet despite the challenges posed by these characteristics, or perhaps because these qualities also provide incentive, adult education researchers and others have been making substantial progress.

Additional incentive is being offered by the elaboration and expansion of programs intended to serve adult needs. The aspiration to provide exemplary programs has focused attention on the limitations of the research results available to help program specialists make sound decisions. Professional adult educators, trainers, and others want to know more about the motives and goals of specific adults; about how adults in certain age ranges handle interpersonal relations and conflicts; about how they can more efficiently and effectively help an adult to develop a new skill or understanding. Others are interested in improving delivery systems and procedures, methods of finance, administrative procedures and the like. The consequences of these developments is clearly a growing demand for more and better information and therefore also for more and better research, using methods specially suited to the study of adults.

Defining Adult Education Research

Definition is a device used to sort things into categories for purposes of identification and communication. The more precise the definition, the greater the restrictions on what can qualify for inclusion in any category and the greater the possibility that different individuals will have the same understanding about the identity of a phenomenon. Mental convergence, then, is assisted by definition and contributes to improved communication. Unfortunately, the term *adult education research* lacks a commonly accepted precise definition. Each word in the term has been variously defined, and perhaps no diverse absolute consensus is possible. Thus, rather than attempt to explicate any of these words, I will merely provide a few examples of definitions and share my own views.

Adult Education. Taking first things first, let us examine what is meant by adult education. Adult education has been both narrowly and broadly defined according to a variety of criteria, from the way it functions to the characteristics of its clients. The interested reader is referred to Verner (1964, p. 30), Schroeder (1970, pp. 25–44) and Spence (1955) for more detailed discussions.

Of the efforts to distinguish adult education from other kinds of education, those of Bryson (1936) and Verner are noteworthy. According to Bryson (1936, pp. 3–4), adult education is all activities with an educational purpose carried on by people in the ordinary business of life who use only *part* of their time and energy to acquire intellectual equipment. Verner's definition (1964, p. 32) is more restrictive: "Adult education is a relationship between an educational agent and a learner in which the agent selects, arranges, and continuously directs a sequence of progressive tasks that provide systematic experience to achieve learning for those whose participation in such activities is subsidiary and supplemental to a primary productive role in society."

I prefer to remove the part-time and agent restrictions and define adult education as any planned learning activity engaged in by and for anyone who possesses the biological, civil, and cultural characteristics of an adult. Admittedly, this definition is extremely broad, but so is the field of adult education. Adding restrictive elements appears to be desirable only when we want to specify certain kinds of adult education activities. Such a procedure parallels the classification system used in biology: education is the kingdom, adult is the phylum; the class, family, genus, and species are to be determined through greater specification.

Research. The definitional range of this word reflects the varying levels of sophistication and complexity of the process and the research experience of the individual using the word. For example, research may be broadly defined to include any procedure used to collect information for the purpose of making a decision. A more precise definition is the careful, disciplined, organized, and exhaustive investigation of all ascertainable evidence bearing on a definable problem (Hillway, 1974, p. 5). Other restrictions also are frequently placed on the definition. Two such limitations concern the generalizability of the findings and the purpose of the inquiry. That is, research findings are expected to be generalizable to large populations or to other similar phenomena, and research consists of inquiries that attempt to assess the scientific truth of a thing as opposed to inquiries designed to evaluate the worth of something (Glass, 1970).

Some writers suggest, however, that the crucial question is not whether or why differences among definitions exist but what, if anything, is common to all the activities defined as research. Thus the answer to the critical question is to be found not in what is studied but in how the inquiry is conducted (Aker and Schroeder, 1969). Research can then be distinguished from other means that are frequently used to answer a question or solve a problem, such as simply letting change occur, adopting trial-and-error procedures, generalizing from experience, or depending on mysticism, tradition, and custom.

To answer the more important questions of reality, mankind has attempted to develop more dependable ways than those noted above to determine truth. Consequently, several methods for determining reality, resolving issues, and answering questions have evolved, including appeals to authority, philosophical and religious systems, and the scientific method. Each has its adherents and detractors, of course, who emphasize either its strengths or weaknesses. Though it is not the purpose of this chapter to examine and discuss the relative merits of the different modes, a few comments drawn from the literature that relate to the issue are included. Other chapters in this book also touch on the reliability and status of different systems of inquiry or problem resolution.

The Scientific Method. This book is concerned with the scientific method of determining what is real as opposed to the other means mentioned above. The scientific method has several definite and identifiable steps: (1) identifying the problem to be investigated, (2) collecting the essential facts related to the problem, (3) developing tentative explanations of the problem, (4) evaluating the explanations to determine their relative congruence with the observations (facts), and (5) selecting the most likely explanation (Hillway, 1974, p. 12). Important assumptions on which scientific research is based are discussed in Chapter Two.

Diverse problems have been solved by the use of the scientific method. In pure research the investigator uses the method to discover new knowledge about the universe. It is used in applied research to develop a new product or process. And recently educators have used the scientific method in what has been labeled action research to resolve practical problems encountered in the learning environment.

Adult educators have found the scientific method helpful in improving the concepts used in the field. For example, until about 1940 many adult educators perceived adult education to be primarily for those people with limited previous educational opportunity. The studies of Boshier (1971), Johnstone and Rivera

(1965), and others have demonstrated overwhelmingly that the reverse is true, that the extent to which people participate in adult education is positively correlated with the level of their educational achievement. Londoner (1974) presents evidence that weakens another previously held assumption, this one concerning the motivations of students whose fees are paid by an agency. His findings cast doubt on the assertions of some administrators that persons who have their fees paid by an agency are unmotivated and generally unresponsive to academic programs in the adult secondary schools and that their main reason for attending is to receive financial aid. Of course, additional study is required to support or refute his findings.

Thus, as the use of the scientific method provides new knowledge, it concomitantly challenges old ideas and thereby makes humans more humble when facing the unknown. No longer are they likely to believe they possess a corpus of absolutely reliable knowledge that will provide complete, authoritative answers to questions. Consequently, contemporary investigators are generally open-minded, for they are aware that revolutionary advances made by science in the past century have challenged and overthrown some long-accepted beliefs. Knowledge of those developments has encouraged a flexible spirit of inquiry that makes it easier to question accepted theories. Furthermore, such a spirit contributes to the investigators' humility, as they recognize that their own discoveries too are fallible.

Research concerning the ability of adults to learn provides a quintessential illustration of the scientific method in action. Beginning with the classic work of E. L. Thorndike and others (1928), a series of investigations spanning more than half a century has answered various questions on this subject. And each major study has tended to generate more positive findings and more generous interpretations concerning the adult's ability to learn.

The scientific method of inquiry is not infallible, nor does it lead to absolute certainty; but it is more reliable than some other means of answering questions, which have been characterized (Cohen and Nagel, 1934, p. 195) as inflexible, as containing no provision for error and correction. The scientific method, in contrast, encourages doubt in order to make sure that what is left after such critical assessment is supported by the best available evidence. In

addition to its fallibility, however, the scientific method has other
limitations. It is slow, it is not a perfect method for discovering
truth, and it is limited in application to certain kinds of questions.
Conant (1947, p. 10) has declared that "only an occasional brave
man will be found nowadays to claim that the so-called scientific
method is applicable to the solutions of almost all the problems of
daily life in a modern world."

The rather lively debates that appear in the learned journals,
including *Adult Education,* reveal the controversy concerning the
scope of the applicability of the scientific method. Some analysts
suggest, for instance, that the scientific method is primarily suited
to the natural sciences and that its use should be limited accordingly.
Others question the concept of a single scientific method. There is
rather general agreement that one cannot establish a single rigid
set of logical rules for natural sciences, anthropology, mathematics,
history, and education. Certainly these fields differ; nevertheless,
they have enough in common to reach a unified scientific approach.

In spite of its limitations, the scientific method is one of the
most promising tools available to humankind to extend the fron-
tiers of knowledge and to increase the accumulation of tested and
verified truth. In the following discussion, therefore, adult education
research is conceptualized as the application of the scientific method
to discovering new knowledge about learners, content, curricula,
activities, institutions, and similar topics of concern to adult educators.

Special Characteristics of Adult Education Research

Just as a range of differences distinguishes research in the
natural sciences from inquiry in the social sciences, so certain special
characteristics of research concerning adult education distinguish it
from other educational research. Investigators seeking to establish a
data base for adult education theory and practice soon become
aware that their research problems are not usually the same as those
faced by other educational researchers. Some of the questions may
be similar, but both the populations and the educational practices
are often sufficiently different from those that most educators and
psychologists study to require modification of the research activities.

I have selected six characteristics of adult-education research to illustrate this idea.

First, research that focuses on the adult period of life is complicated by its relative length, with its attendant variables. Major research issues may easily stretch across a population with a fifty-year range of experience and cultural differences, in contrast to the much more restricted age range studied by other educators. It should be obvious that the challenge of designing appropriate investigations to comprehend such a span of time adequately is not to be taken lightly. The confounding and complex research issues are reflected in one of the oldest subjects of scientific inquiry of interest to adult education, the problem of adult learning ability or adult intelligence. Inquiries on this topic are replete with ambivalent, equivocal, and apparently contradictory results and interpretations. Findings are either supported and explained or discounted by various investigators because they are longitudinal, cross-sectional, or cross-sequential. Each design contains weaknesses that seem to be complicated by the combined length and nature of this life period.

A second distinguishing characteristic is the lack of agreement on what constitutes an adult. This lack of consensus interferes with communication and the interpretation of data. For instance, the differing opinions concerning the rates of participation in adult education activities can be traced directly to this characteristic. Failure to agree on the definition of an adult has contributed to large sample differences, and subsequently to substantial differences among the estimates of participation. Four studies of adult education participation reported in the literature use no fewer than four different definitions of adults. Houle (1973, p. 66) cites an unpublished work of Abraham Carp and Richard Peterson in which they define their subjects as "eighteen through sixty living in their own homes and not in full-time residence at a school or college." Johnstone and Rivera (1965, pp. 31–32) used the following aggregates: "(1) all householders twenty-one years of age or over; or (2) under twenty-one but married; or (3) under twenty-one but the head of a household; plus (4) all persons twenty-one or over who live on an armed forces base and have close family ties with some adult members of an American household; and (5) anyone twenty-one or over and living in a school residence or dormitory and closely related to some household member." Finally, the survey data of the U.S. Office of Education (USOE) cover all participants who are beyond compulsory school age, seventeen or over, who are not enrolled full time in a regular school or college program and are engaged in one or more activities of organized instruction (National Center for Education Statistics, 1975).

Similarly, the third distinguishing characteristic, lack of agreement on the properties of adult education, presents difficulty for the investigator and scholar. The differences among the definitions contribute to difficulties in communicating, comprehending, interpreting, and applying the findings of various studies. For example, Verner's definition of adult education, cited earlier, seems to exclude the self-directed learning activities studied by Tough (1971); hence, using Verner's definition, we would eliminate the independent learner from the concerns of adult education. If people do not agree about what constitutes either an adult or adult education, there is bound to be some disagreement also on what constitutes appropriate inquiry, observation, and interpretation in the field.

A fourth distinguishing characteristics of adult education research relates to questions of ethics and values. For example, investigators who believe that the experimental research method manipulates people and that such manipulation is always inappropriate will need to discover and use different techniques, such as grounded theory. Investigators are thus challenged to test their research objectives against philosophical and ethical principles as well as the canons of logic.

The nature of the samples selected in the study of adult behavior is another element that makes such research distinctive. Investigators interested in adult behavior, like most researchers, have to be concerned with both internal and external validity. The character of the adult population, however, presents particular difficulties. Researchers who seek a "normal" sample have some novel challenges, as do their colleagues who require a homogeneous sample. Because the normal adult population contains persons of widely different behavior, age, background, and so on, it is not easy to obtain what might be considered a normal randomly selected sample. Consequently, researchers often resort to one of two different strategies. They select subjects on the basis of their availability—that is, members of existing groups, clubs, or organizations, and students—or they use extremely small samples. And not infrequently they use both.

An analysis of a sample of eighteen studies using adult subjects reported in volumes 24–27 of *Adult Education* revealed the following. The sample size in the studies ranged from 11 to 728; seven investigations were based on data from 200 or more subjects, and four of the studies had a maximum of 20 subjects. Ten of the samples were composed of students. Nurses made up the sample in three investigations, physical therapists in one, and pharmacists in one. Former prison inmates and the alumni of a graduate program in adult education were the subjects in two studies. Another investigation reported a sample composed of members of six preexisting groups.

If the frequent use of students, health care personnel, and other available clusters of individuals, combined with small samples, is characteristic of adult education research, this phenomenon may threaten the external validity or generalizability of the research. However, new methods of statistical analysis and interpretation may eventually strengthen our confidence in small-sample studies. McKeachie and Kulik (1975) describe one recent innovative procedure referred to as "vote counting" that may interest adult educators. Vote counting is designed to further analyze studies comparing the lecture and discussion methods of college teaching. Using this procedure, McKeachie and Kulik (1975) went beyond an earlier review that considered only the mean score on the final examination. They based their analysis on three criteria: an examination, a measure of retention and higher level thinking, and measures of attitudes and motivation. Disregarding statistical significance levels, they compared the similarities and differences of the two methods. Their results provide a picture different from the one presented by the original analysis, which offered only the statistically significant result. Another procedure that may prove useful to adult education researchers is recommended by Gage (1978). This procedure, attributed to Karl and Egon Pearson, tests the significance of combined results as a way of overcoming some of the effects of small-sample studies.

Diversity, a recognized characteristic of any group of adults, presents a unique contrasting challenge to the person trying to select appropriate samples that will protect the internal validity require- ments of scientific investigations. For example, investigators may find it extremely difficult to obtain a large sample matched on selected characteristics or to obtain the homogenity desired within a specific group of available adults. Faced with such a predicament, investi- gators have only a few options, and according to strict research canons, some of these are not desirable. In such cases researchers may proceed and ignore the question of homogeneity; they may continue the research on the assumption that the members of the sample are similar; they may use a statistical procedure such as analysis of covariance; or researchers may resort to using an ex- tremely small, but matched, sample and run the risk of a "type II error"—failing to reject a null hypothesis that should be rejected.

The significance of this feature of adult-based research may not be readily apparent, however, because of the heavy reliance adult educators have placed on descriptive and correlational studies.

A sixth characteristic arises from the sophistication of an adult sample. Data based on naive responses are difficult to obtain because the educational and occupational experiences of a sizable segment of the available adult population have made them increas- ingly sophisticated or test-wise. Furthermore, investigators realize that adults are more likely than younger respondents to attempt to provide the correct or valued response. For example, I am familiar with a study wherein the adult respondents were requested to de- scribe, first on a written questionnaire and several weeks later in response to in-depth interviews, the leisure activities of their neigh- bors. Not surprisingly, the first set of responses followed certain middle-class family-oriented values, whereas the second set of re- sponses revealed a much wider range of activities.

The Literature

The beginnings of a literature on adult education research can be traced to pre-World War II days; however, the literature of the past twenty-five years is the most pertinent for the purposes of this chapter. Several threads are discernible in the literature. Some writing relates research concerns to graduate instruction. A number of bibliographic works identify the research publications of interest to adult educators. And finally, the more analytical and philosophical literature describes and criticizes the status of adult education research and sometimes comments on what ought to be.

Research and Graduate Study. The limited literature on this aspect of the field suggests that the development of competent researchers is an important goal of graduate work. In the late fifties Whipple (1958) identified a pair of research needs among adult educators: the need to search for truth as scientists and the competing need to improve the practice of adult education. His solution was to separate adult education from the graduate school and make it a professional element in the university structure similar to schools of medicine and law. During the early sixties, as graduate programs in adult education began to proliferate, Liveright (1964) made some observations about the nature and aims of the programs. Drawing on the work of William McGlothlin, he identified five attributes common to all programs of graduate education, one of which was that the graduate should possess enough competence to add to human knowledge through either discovery or the application of new truths. Liveright noted that all professions demand that their graduates will do some kinds of continuing learning and require at least a minimal understanding of relevant research. He then cited the expectations of the medical and social work professions and concluded that adult education "can hardly settle for less than the research requirements established by the medical profession" (p. 99).

Douglah and Moss (1969, p. 132) succinctly stated the relationship between research skills and graduate study:

> The doctoral program should also be concerned with developing considerable competence in research methodology. While this is an obvious need in the case of those whose primary role will be research, it is also important for those whose future roles may be primarily teaching. As professors of adult education, their role will include advising students on research, and thus they, as well as the researcher, will directly affect the quality of adult education research performed. Since it is generally conceded that the development of a field of study is

linked to the quality and quantity of research done, the nature of graduate training in this area should receive attention.

Boyd (1969) took a more controversial position concerning the content of doctoral programs in adult education. He noted that since doctoral programs are directly concerned with adult education as a subject of study, the emphasis should be on research. Boyd noted, "our purpose is to observe, analyze, and develop evidence and theory to explain that which we are examining and studying. If by this process we develop excellent practicing professionals, all to the good. . . . But it must be remembered that this is not our direct goal" (p. 190).

Research training in graduate programs is also recognized as contributing to the professional competence of the adult educator. Aker (1962) and Houle (1970) have commented on that relationship. Even though Houle's analysis of adult education leadership does not specifically cite the performance of competent research as among the four identified functions of leadership, one can infer that such skill is required by individuals who can perform his fourth function, namely, advancing adult education as a field of study. Aker points out a need for greater skill among adult educators in identifying, critically evaluating, and discussing scholarly work by investigators in adult aducation.

Bibliographic Literature. This category contains the greatest number of publications concerned with adult education research, including articles by DeCrow and Loague (1970), Grabowski (1973), Grabowski and Loague (1970), Kaplan (1957), Thiede and Draper (1963, 1964), and Thiede and Meggars (1965, 1966). The bibliographic literature is useful to the field but has limited value in this discussion. I mention it only to assure that the reader is aware of it.

Philosophical and Analytical Literature. Among the contributions to this second-largest body of adult education research literature are those of Bittner (1950), Brunner and others (1959), Essert (1953), Hallenbeck (1964), Hendrickson (1960), Jensen (1964), Kreitlow (1959, 1960, 1964a, 1964b, 1970), Spence

(1953), and Verner (1956). In addition, several complete issues of the *Review of Educational Research* published between 1950 and 1965 focused on adult education. The 1950 and 1960 editions of the *Encyclopedia of Educational Research* and the chapters by Kreitlow (1960, 1970) in the *Handbook of Adult Education* provide a useful profile of the development of adult education research. Those publications, supplemented by Brunner's overview and the comments of Jensen, Liveright, and Hallenbeck in their outlines of the field, provide an excellent base from which to examine how research on and in the field of adult education has grown.

Review of Development

My review begins with an examination of the literature of the early 1950s, considers the predominance of descriptive research, identifies a period of transition in which research activity began to proliferate, and analyzes the dependence of adult education researchers on theory borrowed from the traditional disciplines.

Early Work. The earliest works, cited above, reflect a mixture of concern and optimism as the fledgling field of adult education struggled to establish itself. Each succeeding author generally expresses a little more optimism as research products and skills emerge over the decades. Grabowski's chapter in the present book exemplifies this attitude.

Early editions of the *Review of Educational Research* (Houle, 1953; Spence, 1950) were less optimistic about the status of adult education research than were later descriptions and analyses. In the 1953 *Review*, for example, Houle observed that research had long suffered from a lack of information about activities in the field. In his opinion, even the simplest questions frequently went unanswered. Accordingly, he cited the need for basic bodies of facts that would provide a baseline for progress and a framework for more detailed study. At the same time, however, Houle was heartened by the improving quality of the literature and the increasing trend toward the replacement of conjecture and unfounded assertion by scientific studies and objective data.

Essert (1953), writing in the same issue of the *Review*,

described the period between 1949 and 1952 as a time when adult education was developing the broad outlines of a substantive research program with an increasing base of trained researchers and research funding. He was not completely optimistic, however, noting that with respect to many important questions in adult education there was little evidence of research and experimentation. He observed, for example, that practically no significant research had taken up the problems related to financing adult education. Essert also cited the great need for research in adult education similar to the many studies then being done on the growth and development of children and adolescents.

In the same general period, Bittner (1950) noted the absence of a clear and standard definition of adult education by any large group of investigators or leaders in the "various associated movements" of adult education. He referred to the dearth of basic research in the social sciences by specialists in selected fields such as anthropology, sociology, and social psychology as one reason for the divergence of opinion concerning the definition of adult education. Bittner identified the two publication series sponsored by the American Association for Adult Education, "Studies in Adult Education" and "Studies in the Social Significance of Adult Education in the United States," along with the Report of the Regent's Inquiry, the publications of the Employment Stabilization Institute, and *The Literature of Adult Education,* as examples of some of the better research reports of the period. In conclusion, he predicted that research in adult education would probably continue to be largely descriptive, derivative, philosophical, and markedly applied in its orientation. Bittner gave two reasons for his conclusions: first, the complexity and rapidity of change, and second and more important, adult educators' failure to understand the scientific method and cultural relativity (p. 32).

Approximately ten years later, the study of adult-education research by Brunner and others (1959) noted that "any examination of research in adult education reveals a rather chaotic situation. . . . A few pertinent areas, such as adult learning, have been explored far more thoroughly than others," while "some have received almost no research attention." Furthermore, they observed that, other than in the field of methods, most research of consequence had been conducted by social scientists other than adult educators (p. 2).

Descriptive Research. Kreitlow (1960) followed closely, in time and content, the observations of Brunner and his colleagues. The status of research in adult education was not high, he said, in terms of either amount or quality. He closed the decade with an observation similar to the one Bittner had made ten years earlier: "The last two decades of adult education might be identified as the age of description" (p. 12). But he was not pessimistic about the possible negative effects that the descriptive studies might have on adult education research and, unlike Bittner, did not associate the descriptive studies with any basic conceptual flaw common to adult educators.

Kreitlow's sense of guarded optimism was evident in his writing four years later (1964b), even as he stated that the giant steps needed in adult education research remained to be taken. At that time, he pointed out that even though important contributions had been made, the absence of structure and lack of theory prevented the launching of new research and the integration of previous work. To illustrate the benefits of developing rigorous structures and models in adult education, he pointed to some eminently successful studies of diffusion, innovation, and adoption that were constructed on such foundations.

Later, Kreitlow (1970) indicated that although researchers were still emphasizing "what" rather than "why," he was encouraged by the increasing number and size of graduate programs. Their growth, he felt, indicated greater attention among adult educators to research and theory. Still, he noted that the research beginning to appear was "not in great quantity" nor did it have "any consistent quality" (p. 138), descriptions reminiscent of his 1960 comments.

Transition. If the two decades following World War II can be characterized as an era of descriptive research in adult education, then the era beginning about 1966 can be characterized as the period when such research began to have a real, though still relatively minor, impact on the literature and practice. Most writers cited some forces that they believed had helped to improve adult education research. These positive factors include support from certain foundations (Carnegie, Ford, and Kellogg); the support and encouragement provided by the American Association for Adult Education and the Adult Education Association of the U.S.A.; the development of the periodical *Adult Leadership,* its successor, *Lifelong Learning: The Adult Years,* and the journal *Adult Education;* the expansion of graduate instruction programs in adult education; and the size and the increased significance of the Adult Education Research Conference, a loosely structured organization of adult educators interested in research who meet annually to present and discuss their research.

At the same time, other influences have impeded the development of research. These factors include the pressures of practice, the youthfulness of the field, the variety of institutional bases, the traditional emphasis on descriptive studies, and limited theory. The pressures of practice have frequently been noted in the literature. Jensen (1964) likened them to the pressures experienced in engineering, law, medicine, business and public administration, social work, public health, and various other professions whose primary objective is coping with some unsatisfactory condition or problem. In the earlier years of development, adult educators were, perhaps out of necessity, more concerned about what worked than about why something was effective.

This practical thrust, the emphasis on doing instead of investigating or contemplating, not only affected the character of the early literature but probably continues to influence contemporary development as well. Hallenbeck (1964) described knowledge as consisting of three elements—experience, research, and theory—which came into existence in that order. This sequence seems to hold true for adult education knowledge.

The tendency to do, then report, generated a number of personal narratives that lacked a high degree of generalizability. The next developmental step was the publication of numerous status reports and other descriptive studies. The movement from the experience-based personal reports to descriptive studies was a natural and orderly development because of the close relationship between description and practice. The limited generalizability and application of much of the early research was due partly to the complications caused by the variety of institutions in which adult education programs are located and to inadequate research designs. This period of transition will end when a sufficient number of graduates of adult education graduate programs have assumed responsibility for the literature of their field.

Dependence on Other Disciplines. Adult educators have generally looked to other disciplines for their theoretical foundations. As Jensen (1964) and the Commission of the Professors of Adult Education (1961) noted, adult education has been advanced through the borrowing and adapting of knowledge, theory, and research technology from other fields. While acknowledging this dependence, however, the Commission cautioned that not all material from the social sciences is appropriate to adult education and suggested that adult education should not only test the applicability of existing knowledge but discover for itself new knowledge or new relationships within existing knowledge. According to the Commission members, adult education is original in developing special knowledge about the unique characteristics of adults as learners. Yet, the development of adequate knowledge about adults as learners and about the administration of adult learning opportunities requires the involvement of far more researchers than the relatively few who are now identified directly with the field of adult education. They also stated that our knowledge of adult education is limited because subjects of interest to adult educators were often of secondary interest to other educators and social scientists and because there was no mechanism for systematically planning, stimulating and disseminating adult education research.

The dependence of adult education on other fields within education and on the social sciences for research and theory came about for several reasons. First, for a fledgling field, it made sense to use the knowledge developed by one's parents and relatives. And second, of course, the early professors had to come from somewhere, and in this case somewhere was usually education and the social sciences. Third, because the group of scholars involved was quite small—only twenty-four professors were listed on the Commission's 1961 roster, for instance—their resources were necessarily spread very thinly.

Another probable cause was the great diversity of the field. Indeed, Kreitlow asked in 1960 whether this diversity was such that research might always have to be borrowed. Although Kreitlow probably then considered a negative answer possible, believing that the borrowing might continue only until adult education was more clearly defined, in 1975 when he spoke at a panel session at the Adult Education Research Conference, he seemed to have accepted the view that adult education would primarily build on a foundation of research in the social science disciplines by interpreting its implications for adult education. The suggestion made by the Commission of Professors—that the unique characteristics of adults as learners could and should be the focus of original research— appears to have been overlooked by those who were conducting research on teaching, learning, and administration of adult education. Or attitudes had changed in the interim.

Mezirow (1971), however, took a different position concerning the borrowing and adaptation. He indicated that adult education should have its own theoretical structure based on research. He further speculated that in the absence of theories suited to adult education as a professional field, research efforts had been fragmented. Mezirow described most of the research as (1) atheoretical or factual, (2) conceptual, (3) organizing or critically evaluating existing factors, or (4) designed to test logical deductions from assumptions, general formulations either from the literature or from some element of formal theory couched in other disciplines.

Thus, from about 1950 through 1970 much of the literature presented adult education research as an adaptation of work in the social sciences. Only a few voices were raised to argue for the development of theory that would be unique to adult education.

Newer Approaches to Research. Since the early seventies, when Kreitlow and Mezirow stated their positions, others have offered differing opinions about the nature of adult education research. Reflecting a concern similar to Kreitlow's, Beder and Darkenwald (1974) picked up Whipple's theme (1958) and described adult education as an applied professional field. As such, it needs two different kinds of studies: basic research designed to extend knowledge and theory and, equally important, research intended to help solve problems of policy and practice.

Apps (1972) called for a broader definition of research, one that moves beyond empirical inquiry. According to Apps, adult educators have been caught up in believing that all knowledge comes from empirical research. Accordingly, he encouraged the consideration of other paths to knowledge such as thinking, synthesizing, sensing, and accepting—or, in Royce's terms (1964), rationalism, intuitionism, empiricism, and authoritarianism, respectively. Addressing himself to empiricism, Apps noted that a ritualistic approach to empirical research could be particularly limiting. "Insistence on rigor as defined by a right adherence to a ritualistic method may close off many sources of insight and information" (p. 63).

Forest (1972) joined Apps in criticizing scientific empiricism in adult education research. His main contention was that scientific empiricism is viewed as the only legitimate approach to research and that such a position is hindering the development and application of other kinds of research. For example, Forest encouraged the greater acceptance of subjects' personal reports and an increased use of systematic and logical analysis. He concluded that an overwhelming emphasis on empiricism in adult education has stifled equally legitimate and worthwhile avenues of research that may be able to cope with questions which cannot be answered through empirical research.

Shillace (1973), following Apps and Forest, argued for balancing the need for rigor in scientific study with the need to consider interest. He claims that many adult educators find scientific study too rigorous, too limited in its opportunities for creativity and innovation. Consequently, he opts for more of what he describes as high-risk research.

The statements by Apps, Forest, and Shillace appear to be calling for a return to the kind of descriptive, personal-report research which characterized adult education in the earlier years and which, contrary to their remarks, has continued to be a hallmark of most adult education research.

Reviews of the publications of adult educators do not generally support the charge that adult education is overly empirical. Long and Agyekum (1974), having analyzed *Adult Education* over a nine-year period, 1964–1973, concluded that approximately 60 percent of the articles were descriptive statements of personal belief, and program descriptions. Dickinson and Rusnell's similar analysis (1971), this one covering a twenty-year period, 1950–1970, indicated that only 22 percent of the articles were based on empirical research. Furthermore, 48 percent were reporting on descriptive surveys. Thus, these analyses indicate that while empirical studies may have increased recently, such inquiry methods do not yet dominate the practice of research. Apps and others may have gained their impressions from hearing repeated assertions of the need for empirical studies.

Although this literature review has focused on research methods, at least one observation needs to be made concerning research topics. Kreitlow (1975), having reviewed the topics studied between 1964 and 1975, noted that unfortunately very little progress had been made in addressing the questions he had identified as priorities in 1963–64. His explanations for this limited progress suggest that adult educators responded to pressures from university administrators and federal grants. Responsiveness to funding agencies and organization leaders in identifying research problems leads to a great deal of activity but does not seem to yield much in the way of additions to the fundamental knowledge of the field. Action research in adult education has not been of much value in the advancement of theory.

To sum up, then: adult education research has been influenced by a number of factors over the past fifty years. Some of those factors have encouraged improved inquiry; others have retarded it. Positive forces such as an increase in the number of doctoral students, the stimulation provided by the increasing stability of the Adult Education Research Conference, the availability of a research publication outlet in the form of *Adult Education,* and a slowly accumulating body of knowledge that is expanding in depth and breadth are contending with the negative pressures of a practice-oriented discipline, the immaturity of the field, and some confusion about the source and existence of theoretical foundations in adult education. In spite of, or perhaps because of, these opposing forces, adult education research is slowly coming of age. This publication is one of the events in its evolution. It is significant that interest in adult education research has reached a level to justify the discussion of the various topics included in the following chapters.

Chapter Two

Basic Elements in Planning and Practicing Research

Huey B. Long
Roger Hiemstra

In this chapter we are concerned with practical matters rather than with the philosophical and theoretical issues to which the other chapters are addressed. Our primary purpose is to help the novice researcher, or graduate student, plan, practice, and report research. But even though the chapter focuses on procedures for organizing and pursuing a research question at a basic level—specifically, with developing theses and dissertations—we have also identified certain properties common to the planning and practice of many kinds of research, commonalities that should make the chapter instructive to a variety of individuals, not only to students but to administrators, to staff members of agencies who are interested in problem-solving research related to the agency's mission, and to people in government bureaus and special research institutes. Accordingly, we discuss some basic characteristics of research being done in the numerous adult education graduate programs, describe a few of the expectations professors of adult education have concerning research, and share a few writing tips.

The major commonalities discussed in the following pages are the research needs of both adult educators and the field of adult education, the approach to research, and the preparation of a proposal and a dissertation.

Research Needs of Adult Educators

Educators generally agree that graduate study should contribute to one's research competence, competence that is achieved through a combination of academic experiences, including formal courses on such topics as statistics, research methodology, and computer science. However, such courses in themselves are incomplete, and thus the skills and knowledge acquired in them must be integrated in another framework. Formal research, as required for a thesis or dissertation, provides that integrative framework wherein the student can learn to develop proposals, work out strategies for analyzing and interpreting data, and practice report writing.

Besides competence, graduate students also need an awareness of their assumptions and biases, and doing research should help them develop this. One of the important assumptions they should recognize, even if it is not stated by many of the researchers who hold it, is that past events in nature will recur provided similar circumstances exist again. Even more strongly held is the belief that such events must happen if identical circumstances prevail. From these basic assumptions about the uniformity and orderliness of nature have arisen three postulates: the postulates of natural kinds, constancy, and determinism, each of which is briefly discussed later in the chapter. For a more detailed discussion, the reader should consult some works on the philosophy of science, such as Cohen and Nagel (1934).

The postulate of natural kinds is as old as Aristotle. It refers to the possibility of classifying phenomena according to similarities among their essential structures, functions, or characteristics. Such activity leads to the development of classes, categories, and taxonomies which help the researcher bring some order to what may appear to be chaotic masses of data. Verner's work (1964) provides an example of the postulate specifically applied to adult education. Other useful examples include the Linnaean classification system in botany, the periodic table in chemistry, and Bloom's taxonomy of educational objectives (Bloom and others, 1956).

Another important postulate that undergirds most research is that of constancy. Although researchers do not often find opportunities to expound on this postulate, it is significant because it suggests that natural phenomena are sufficiently stable to maintain essential attributes under given conditions or circumstances for a stated period of time. The postulate of constancy implies relative persistence and organization in nature.

And according to the third basic postulate, determinism, all natural phenomena are determined, that is, they are caused by some agent or event. The determinist rules out chance and accident as legitimate causes. An experiment designed to predict a phenomenon clearly depends on this postulate. So the researcher, especially the graduate student, needs to be aware of the premises underlying his efforts.

The practice of research at the graduate level also contributes to an understanding of theory and its role in research. Theory relates to inquiry in two distinct ways: deductively and inductively. When theory is the point of departure for the investigation, research proceeds deductively, usually by testing hypotheses. In the second way, observation and inductive analysis contribute to the evolvement of theory. The experimental research design is most often theory-based and tests various parts of a specific theory deductively. In contrast, the grounded-theory research strategy generates conclusions or hypotheses that may contribute to the development of theory.

Because of various professional needs of the adult educator, requiring him or her to do graduate research is a reasonable proposition (Aker, 1962). Many persons enter the field of adult education following practice in another field. And since often the jobs they take in the field do not require an advanced degree, these entrants frequently have had a good deal of practical experience but limited academic preparation. Consequently, they probably lack appreciation not only for the theory and philosophy of adult education but for research theories and methods. The adult educator must be a pragmatic philosopher and a philosophical pragmatist. Such a role derives great strength from experience in research.

Furthermore, we dispute the claim that it is either desirable or wise to separate research from practice. In the broadest sense we see all adult educators as practicing researchers and research-oriented practitioners. The roles are complementary, and efforts to divide them yield sour fruit. Although in a narrower sense, some adult educators produce more research than others and some consume more than others, most will be engaged in research to some degree. Such research may not be as formally organized and as complex as that done for a dissertation; it may be simply the orderly treatment of data to answer questions. Yet even when it takes this simplified form, the researcher is confronted with concerns about spurious data and validity. And if the adult educator is primarily a consumer of research, he still needs at least a basic understanding of the inquiry process and of how to critically evaluate studies conducted by others.

Thus all adult educators, including those whose functions do not involve the practice of formal research, can profit from research training at the graduate level. Even an individual who consistently avoids all semblance of overt data collection, if there be such a person, is influenced by the research of others. The practitioner who narrowly limits his attention to doing things and does not read research reports is still affected by research, because funds are sometimes appropriated as a result of research findings, and such appropriations may strengthen or weaken a specific adult education program. Though some adult educators may never write a research publication after they have obtained their doctorates, it is difficult to imagine their completely withdrawing from reading. Complete withdrawal is about the only way to escape reading about some kind of research, even if the reports are just polls published in the newspapers or popular magazines.

Thus far we have discussed how research training can help to satisfy some of the adult educator's professional needs. To close this section we want to point out another need: to consult with other specialists. Such consultation is often productive, as it brings the adult educator into contact with scholars from other disciplines or into closer contact with other adult educators with different interests and skills. Other specialists not only have different ways of asking research questions but also they utilize different methods of gathering, analyzing, and interpreting evidence. Either kind of experience should be valuable to both parties as well as to the field of adult education, in which diversity is necessary. Just as it would be restrictive for all researchers concerned with questions related to adult education to subscribe to identical research methods, so would it be undesirable for all researchers to specialize in one kind of data analysis. Fortunately, such a prospect is unlikely. The analysis, like the research method, should be appropriate to the question, the sample, and the design.

Research Needs of the Field

Since graduate programs are a major stimulus to adult education research, the continued development of the field is related to the quality of graduate research activities. Those activities potentially have both a short-run and a long-run value. The short-term benefit derives from the immediate production of research and its subsequent contribution to knowledge and practice. The long-term benefit is the collection of research skills that the graduate can apply to adult education questions for years after he leaves the university.

The preceding view places a pragmatic value on graduate research and the skills developed by the experience. As noted by Long in Chapter One, individuals whose professional responsibilities include the planning and delivery of a variety of service programs represent a range of interests and needs. Graduate instruction should be broad enough to help develop the philosophy, skill, and knowledge necessary to meet many of those needs. It would seem that Jensen's five characteristic needs of adult educators (1964, pp. 106–107) are shared by many other people in the helping professions who do not strictly consider themselves to be adult educators and that all these individuals require a basic research competence to perform their occupational tasks. For example, Jensen defines the need to be able to analyze a variety of factors and make competent decisions—skills that are required and enhanced by the practice of research.

Thus, the justification for the university requirement that adult education students develop research skills is clear. If the adult educator is to be professionally competent, it is highly desirable, if not absolutely necessary, that he have such abilities. Similarly, such capacities seem to be required among the professional leaders in the field if adult education is to continue to develop as a field of practice.

Approach to Research

What are the structural outlines of the research process? What are the skills to be practiced? Although researchers in adult education would undoubtedly provide different specific answers to these questions, certain areas of agreement are general enough to warrant discussion here. Even so, we want to emphasize the general nature of this discussion, lest the reader develop the idea that there is universal agreement on the following structural elements: selecting the problem, stating the problem, reviewing the literature, and designing the research.

Selecting the Problem. This phase is often a period of struggle in which the budding researcher—a student or agency employee—struggles to find a suitable topic. In the selection process some are highly promiscuous, entranced by a different topic daily. Other novices choose a topic so broad that the narrowing process is both painful and difficult. Sometimes the researcher-to-be is spared this dissonance: the major advisor or employer assigns the topic.

Most adult education professors encourage students to select their own topic, giving them a great deal of freedom and responsibility. In the case of an employee, the problem to be studied may be dictated by circumstance as well as by a supervisor's directive. And the research problem may differ from that given to or chosen by the student in being more practical, that is, concerned with obtaining sufficient evidence to continue, discontinue, or modify a program.

Almost any topic can be worthwhile *provided the problem is defined adequately.* Conversely, almost any subject might be unacceptable if the problem is inadequately posed, if an improper conceptual framework is used, or if the boundaries of the research are inappropriate. Novice researchers are frequently impatient with the identification process, and their problems are poorly conceived. They fail to state the problem clearly, overlook major variables, select a problem beyond their capacity to handle, or lack a sound theoretical framework (Van Dalen, 1973).

The identification and selection of research problems require sufficient intelligence to isolate and understand the elements contributing to that selection. And the investigator should ask numerous questions, including personal ones, before he finally selects the problem. The following have been suggested by Van Dalen (1973):

—Is the investigator really interested in the problem but free from strong biases?

—Does the investigator possess the necessary skills, abilities, and background knowledge to study this problem?

—Does the investigator have access to the necessary equipment, space, and subjects to conduct the investigation?

—Will solving the problem contribute to knowledge in the field?

—What kind of application may be made of the findings?

—Are the research tools and techniques sufficiently refined and reliable for the conclusions of the investigation to be of value?

—Will the investigation contribute to the development of other studies?

One good rule for researchers to follow, if they can, is to pick a topic of great interest to them. It may be related to a burning question they have had but heretofore had always been reluctant to ask. It may emerge from their past work or educational experience. It could evolve out of the graduate training experience. It could focus on some problem that the student believes can be solved through adult education. Or perhaps it is directly related to a program of an agency or institution.

We also suggest that researchers pick a topic closely related to their future goals. Ample reasons exist for choosing a topic that may stimulate professional development, such as by contributing knowledge to a specialized area or by building a reputation for skill in a certain subject. There is some danger, perhaps, in being conspicuously opportunistic; but why select a topic in which no one is interested? Topic selection, doubtlessly, is related to how widely read the researcher is, for this is not a sterile, isolated process. It is helped along by experience, by observation, and by a review of the literature. The literature can reveal what kinds of questions others are asking as well as what areas are being neglected. (We return to the literature review later in this chapter.)

An additional observation is that the selection of the research topic can reveal both the maturity and the competence of the student. If the student is too limited in experience, maturity, or exposure to the field, he may fail to recognize many of the significant problems to which research may provide solutions. At the same time, if the person has poor skills, he may be unable to choose wisely among the problems to be studied. Given either circumstance, the investigator probably is not yet ready to pursue a thesis or dissertation problem (Hillway, 1974).

Cohen and Nagel (1934) have suggested that the ability to perceive in an experience the basis of a problem whose resolution contributes to the solution of other problems is not a common talent. The difficulty rests in part in the absence of any standard procedure which can be followed by an individual who wishes to ask significant questions. These authors also noted that a problem cannot even be stated unless the investigator is familiar with the subject matter of the problem.

Stating the Problem. After the investigator has determined that the problem to be studied has enough social value to warrant the research and is sure that his personal skills are sufficient to handle it, the researcher has to state the problem effectively. Before meaningful inquiry can begin, some limitations must be imposed on it. In the very early stages of inquiry the research problem may be broad and vague. But at some point, arrived at through continuous revision, the problem must be sharply focused. Global problems can not be solved in a general fashion. The researcher must state the problem so that it is manageable. Cole and Glass (1977), Long (1977), and Pennington and Green (1976) provide acceptable illustrations of problem statements in which the purpose of the study is explicit.

Two procedures will help the researcher develop the problem statement. As the objective of the statement is to make the topic very specific, the investigator may ask, What do I have to discover? Precisely what problem do I want to solve? Cole and Glass (1977, p. 76) seemed to follow this strategy: "The purpose of this experimental study was to determine the effects of adult participant involvement in program planning on the dependent variables of achievement, information, retention and attitude." The other procedure is to turn the topic into a question instead of a statement. In this form, it requires a specific answer, and then finding the answer becomes the purpose of the study (Hillway, 1974). In the Cole and Glass example, the investigators could easily have asked, Is participation in program planning related to achievement, information, retention, and attitude? Or, Will the presence of participant involvement in program planning affect achievement, information, retention, and attitude?

The evolution of the problem statement is likely to vary among individuals according to personal characteristics that influence their mode of thinking. However, regardless of the procedures, each individual must eventually reduce the problem to dimensions that can be understood, communicated, and organized. The researcher who cannot describe and delimit the task in parsimonious terms will experience difficulty in completing the study.

The problem statement should contain action words that are clear and that can be implemented unambiguously. Words that are easily understood include mathematical *relationships, differences, results,* and *change*. Words that can cause problems, and that usually require careful operational definitions, include *characteristics, analysis,* and *examine*. Several sources, especially Hillway (1974), Kerlinger (1967), Tuckman (1972), and Van Dalen (1973), provide valuable discussions on how to develop problem statements and write operational definitions.

In summary, here are four rules that should be helpful in determining the final definition of a problem:

1. The problem selected should be neither too vague nor too broad in scope.
2. It should be stated as a question that requires a definite answer.

3. The limit and scope of the problem should be carefully stated to eliminate all elements that will not be considered in the study.
4. All the special terms that are used in the problem statement should be defined.

Reviewing the Literature. We cannot overstress the need to review carefully the literature related to a research topic. The task is too often approached too hastily. A thorough review can provide an understanding of the significance of the problem in relation to theory, some clues to appropriate design and methods, and a feeling for how the research will extend knowledge on a given topic. The value of the hours spent in the library is difficult to estimate, but suffice it to observe that such time is usually well spent. Knowing what is already known about a subject is both a necessary step in research and an index to the quality of the forthcoming study. The literature search, however, is complicated by the rapid expansion of information that characterizes many fields. As a result, the reviewer may have difficulty providing a thorough and succinct summary. Nonetheless, the researcher is challenged to become familiar with the appropriate literature in order to accomplish several objectives. The most obvious one is to determine whether the problem or question has already been resolved. A second objective is to obtain helpful ideas concerning the topic. And a third is to find appropriate research procedures.

An important beginning step for the researcher is to become familiar with the various sources of potentially useful information: journals, indexes, periodic literature, government publications, *Dissertation Abstracts,* and the Educational Resources Information Center (ERIC) materials are only a few of the sources to be explored. University library staffs can help the reviewer find and use such materials.

The traditional hand search recently has been augmented if not replaced by the computer search. In many ways the two methods are similar. Both require the early determination of key words on which the search might be focused, and the title of the research or the research problem serves as a good source of key words in either kind of search.

The first item on the form requesting a computer search used by one university requires the investigator to provide a concise statement of what he wants to know. For example, "I am interested in the relationship between dogmatism and learning among adults." The next step is to divide the statement into logical groups stripped of adjectives, conjunctions, and unnecessary modifiers. In the present example, there are three logical groups or concepts: 1. dogmatism, 2. learning, 3. adults. These concepts are connected with *and* logic. That is, the investigator wants to retrieve citations on dogmatism *and* learning *and* adults, not all citations on dogmatism or learning or adults. He wants only citations indexed by all three concepts together. The investigator also indicates the data base or bases to be searched. In the present example the person may request a search of *Psychological Abstracts* and ERIC. Searches may be either retrospective or limited to current materials. (Additional information on computer searches may be obtained from ERIC and universities that provide the service.)

Some investigators combine the hand search and the computer search at one or more stages of the process. A preliminary hand search may be helpful in selecting key words and identifying potential data bases. The hand search procedure may also supplement the computer procedure after pertinent publications have been identified and reported.

The careful recording of information is crucial to success. Complete bibliographic information, key quotations, paraphrased statements, and some individual coding system indicating the potential use of the material are some of the points to consider. Certainly this labor is time consuming. And a large share of the information recorded will not be used in the literature-review section of the research report. But a thorough review should enlarge the researcher's appreciation and understanding of the problem, and the result will be a more educative research experience. Most important, the only way the student can fully comprehend the theoretical basis of the problem is to do a thorough review.

The focus of the literature review may vary according to the research design. For example, if an experimental research design is proposed, the investigator will want to find information concerning theory, previous research findings, and research method, in order to develop a conceptual framework. In contrast, for a study with a historical design the review may be limited to investigating the general outlines of the question or topic. The bulk of such an examination may be simply a listing of the sources to be used in the study.

Selecting the Research Design. Many publications provide guidance in determining what kinds of designs are appropriate for different kinds of research questions. Rather than relist publications cited elsewhere in this book, we refer the reader to the References (Adams and Preiss, 1960; Bledsoe, 1972; Borgatta and Bohrnstedt, 1970; Campbell and Stanley, 1963; Denzin, 1970; McCall and Simmons, 1969; Rosenberg, 1968; Schatzman and Strauss, 1973; Selltiz and others, 1959; Tuckman, 1972; Phillips, 1971). What more should be said to the beginning researcher who is trying to choose an appropriate design? It is that *appropriateness* is the key word. The other chapters in this book should provide the novice with an appreciation for the unique qualities of different research approaches suited to the broad field of adult education.

Appropriateness also implies consistency. In other words, certain problems may be best solved only by certain designs. The unique relationship between the research problem and the research design needs to be reflected in the research proposal. Moreover, researchers should employ a design which is appropriate to their individual abilities and preferences. Although professional consultants are usually available, the researchers themselves may need to defend their choice of design.

New researchers tend to fail in their preliminary conceptualizations of the data that will result from their plan. They create elaborate schemes without considering what the data will look like. Frequently, those researchers are surprised after months of work to find that they have masses of data they cannot use or, equally devastating, inadequate data on important parts of the study.

Therefore we encourage researchers to visualize their data and to project possible outcomes. These two processes are different but related. The first step is to ask questions like these: What will the data look like? Are they in quantifiable form or are they qualitative? Are they nominal? Continuous? Ordinal? Do they fit the statistical analysis selected? The second step is to consider all the possible results. Although hypotheses and theoretical considerations may suggest one particular result, several may be possible. In many studies, for example, at least four outcomes are possible. If the researcher has not considered each of these, he has probably failed to conceive the theoretical dimensions of the study adequately.

Most graduate programs in adult education include courses in statistics and research design. Astute graduate students will enroll in these courses early in their programs, since an understanding of research design and parametric and nonparametric statistics will prove valuable for most researchers. Even those who turn to histor- ical research may find a knowledge of quantitative research helpful. However, if students are to become serious historians, the appropriate historiography courses should be taken. A good graduate program will provide students with ample opportunity to practice research skills before the major test of the dissertation arrives. In assigning preliminary research papers, professors should require writers to follow good writing style and bibliographic style. Such writing should be subjected to adequate reviews and criticisms to acquaint students with their weaknesses and strengths.

The expansion of knowledge and the development of new research tools present a continuing challenge to all scholars. Advanced students and professors engaged in studying adult behavior are challenged to improve their competence by adding new skills as research developments proceed. The procedures of statistical analysis and the application of computer technology to such analysis are two subjects that are changing rapidly.

How much skill and knowledge of statistical procedures constitutes the minimum for adult education researchers? A conversation with three or more experts in experimental design and statistical analysis is likely to reveal different preferences with regard to statistical analyses. One likes analysis of variance, another a correlation technique, and a third a factor analysis for the same set of data. If the experts disagree, what options are available to the novice? As few adults can be specialists in three fields—statistics, computer technology, and adult education—the researcher should probably try to develop above-average competence with the particular statistical technique that seems best suited to the individual's research interests. For many adult education studies nonparametric statistical techniques are more appropriate than parametric ones because of the different assumptions of each and the nature of adult education samples.

Preparing the Proposal

The first tangible activity leading to the dissertation is the preparation of a prospectus, or research proposal. It is often initiated when the student is beginning the last third of the course work. However, students should not delay all consideration of the project until that time. They should give considerable thought to the topic while they are developing research skills, writing ability, and a knowledge of their area of interest, in order to formulate the problem statement.

The prospectuses vary among institutions from brief, informal, general research plans to formal and detailed descriptions of research procedure. Regardless of the institutional requirements, however, the quality of the prospectus is obviously related to the quality of the completed dissertation. Simply stated, the prospectus describes what the student proposes to do, why he proposes to do it, where and when he proposes to do it, with whom he proposes to accomplish the task, and how the tasks will be accomplished. The prospectus should be more than an essay outlining the general problem to be investigated. It should be a highly specific document that requires the student to give critical attention to the problem before conducting research on it. The more attention the student pays to detail in the prospectus, the fewer difficulties she will encounter when she begins collecting data.

The proposed research may take several forms: a case study, a historical analysis, the development of an instrument, descriptive research, or an experimental study. The following outline of the items to be covered in a prospectus constitutes a guide to what the faculty of one adult education department expects when the prospectus is based on an experimental design. Modifications of the outline may be required for students proposing to use the case-study or historical method. However, we believe the general model is appropriate to these methods.

Conceptual Framework. First the writer explicates the relationship among the elements of the study—the problem, the theoretical base, and the research procedures. Since this conceptual framework is frequently based on assumptions that have to be explicitly recognized, the writer presents the major premises underlying the chosen design, sample, and instruments.

Definition of Terms. The writer should use regular terminology whenever possible, keeping jargon to a minimum. Because a term may have several meanings, only one of which is intended within a single statement of an hypothesis, the writer needs to tell the reader exactly which meaning of the term is intended. The writer may also need to formulate operational definitions for certain words. For example, *educational achievement* may be defined in terms of a score on an instrument, or of years of education, or of degrees held. Similarly, what constitutes an adult has been defined differently in various studies, as Long pointed out in Chapter One. So the investigator must be careful to specify what he means.

Statement of the Hypotheses. An experimental study must have hypotheses, preferably stated in the null form. The level of statistical significance required to reject the null hypotheses should also be noted at this point. (For additional comments on hypotheses, see Long's chapter on experimental research.)

Selection of the Sample. The writer relates the selection of his population to the theoretical framework and also indicates the method used to select the sample. For example, if the proposed sample is a random sample, how was randomization established? If the subjects will constitute a fortuitous sample, what led to the selection of the fortuitous sample?

Among the first problems that confront the researcher concerning the sample is the kind of compromise to be made. The investigator has limited resources; hence, everything about every person cannot be observed and recorded. The researcher must decide not only what to observe and record but how many subjects are to be included in the observation. The longitudinal compromise favors the intensive study of a few individauls (Bledsoe, 1972). Tough's work on adults' learning projects (1971) provides an example of a longitudinal compromise in adult education. And Allerton's investigation (1974) based on Tough's work is even more

intensive. We use the word *compromise* because the researcher is
interested in generalizability, and large samples, other things being
equal, are superior to small samples in terms of external validity.
(See the chapters by Long and Boyd for additional comments on
internal and external validity.)

Data Collection. In this section the researcher states in step
fashion how the data will be collected. For example, after selecting
the sample, the writer may develop a control group and an experimental group. In this part of the proposal he discusses how he will
assign subjects to each group, what kind of treatment schedule
will be followed, and how the data will be collected. Clear descriptions of the procedures are essential if readers are to comprehend
exactly what is planned.

Instruments. The investigator provides a section describing
the instruments to be used. For example, if the student plans to use
Rokeach's dogmatism scale, she should briefly describe the instrument, tell how it was developed, and state how the reliability and
validity of the instrument were established (unless the validity and
reliability were discussed in the literature review section).

Treatment of Data. The statistical techniques to be used to
treat the data are a highly important element and should also be
included in the prospectus. The appropriate statistical treatment
should be chosen before any data are collected.

Other Information. The proposal writer often includes a
projected schedule for conducting and reporting the research.
Establishing deadlines beforehand is desirable because they give
the researcher goals he can work toward in certain phases of
the data collection. The investigator should also note various possible
expenses—such as the cost of travel to collect data, the cost of
purchasing and duplicating instruments, and postage—and show
how these will be covered.

Policy on Human Research. As the number and scope of
research studies have increased, researchers have probed ever deeper
and occasionally threatened and or insulted their subjects. At the
same time, people have became more sophisticated in their reactions
to scientific work, more concerned about the moral and ethical implications. Thus, because of the potential danger that some research
with human subjects poses and because of new demands that in-

vestigators be accountable, the federal government has adopted regulations concerning such research. These regulations require universities, and other organizations and institutions that obtain federal funds, to adopt a set of guidelines for monitoring human research. All individuals conducting studies using human subjects should be aware of the policies and guidelines of their institution.

Policies concerning the use of human subjects should be in line with the American Psychological Association's "Ethical Standards in Research," the World Medical Association's Declaration at Helsinki, and the "Institutional Guide to Department of Health, Education and Welfare Policy on Protection of Human Subjects." One such institutional policy (University of Georgia, 1975) lists fifteen different guidelines, having to do with the scientific justification for the research, the qualifications of the investigators, the expected benefits, the protection of the subject, the confidentiality of personal data, informed consent, the protection of individuals not able to exercise fully their powers of choice, and the responsibilities of the researcher to the subject.

Review procedures usually require the investigator to file appropriate documents with the institution or agency for review according to established practice. Several options are available to the review committees: They may approve the request, ask for additional information or clarification, or refuse to approve such research. The time required for review will vary among agencies and institutions; therefore, the researcher should become aware of institutional practices and include sufficient time for the review in the research schedule.

Preparing the Dissertation

The dissertation is often viewed as the final hurdle, the professor's last claim on the student, the last academic ritual before graduation. Such views are unfortunate, because the writing of a dissertation should be a highly constructive educational experience that sharpens the skills of the student-researcher, influences attitudes, and contributes to knowledge. If these kinds of views prevail, the experience will probably lack such favorable characteristics. An overemphasis on the contribution that a dissertation may make to expanding knowledge may also limit the impact that the experience has on the student's development. But with proper balance, there is no reason why the dissertation should not be a valuable learning experience that also contributes to knowledge.

The dissertation may be the key to the writer's future. Either the topic or the research design employed may yield opportunities for recognition and professional development. We know several people who were recruited for good jobs and for consulting work as a direct result of their dissertation research.

Outline. Here is a typical outline for a dissertation:

Acknowledgments
Table of Contents
List of Tables
Chapter 1—Introduction
   A.   Statement of the Problem
   B.   Significance of the Problem
   C.   Review of Related Research
   D.   Summary
Chapter 2—Research Design and Methods
   A.   Conceptual Framework
   B.   Data-Collection Procedures
   C.   Treatment of Data
   D.   Summary
Chapter 3—Presentation of Findings
Chapter 4—Conclusion
   A.   Summary
   B.   Conclusions
   C.   Implications (of findings for practice and theory)
   D.   Recommendations for Further Research
Appendix
References

Style. Writing and bibliographic styles vary among institutions and according to the research methods employed. For example, history is usually written in a more narrative style than are experimental reports. Different institutions and different approaches may dictate both the writing style and bibliographic style.

There is a growing preference for the bibliographic styles used in the older and better established social sciences. The *Pub-*

lication Manual of the American Psychological Association (American Psychological Association, 1974) is a good example of such a style guide. Writers of history and others in the social sciences frequently follow Turabian (1970), while some universities have their own style manuals. Graduate students should become acquainted early with the requirements and expectations of their institution.

Even though institutions differ on bibliographic style, they generally agree that the prose should be accurate, clear, concise, and grammatically correct. Strunk and White (1965) have published a popular guide that struggling writers will find helpful.

There is no reason that a successful dissertation or research report has to be boring. Chambers (1960) has suggested that such a flaw is due only to the ineptitude of the writer or his indifference to the art of communication. Good writing is helpful at every stage of the research process.

Continuing the Process

The feeling of success which accompanies the completion of a dissertation is heady wine. Yet too many graduates in adult education fail to move beyond that first experience in rigorous research. Why? The failure of a large percentage of the more than 1800 adult educators who hold the doctorate to continue their research and writing is a major problem that may stem from a variety of causes. One possible explanation may be the student's attitude toward research, which is often considered mystical or overly abstract and useless in practice. The problem is compounded when the dissertation is viewed as a hurdle rather than as a way of seeking answers. As a result of such negative perceptions, a large number of the doctorates in adult education may be awarded to recipients who vow, "Never again."

The development of this attitude might be prevented if the student's advisory committee would attempt to stimulate curiosity, encourage observation, foster inquiry, and then provide ample nonthreatening opportunities for the prospective adult educator to test his ability to use a variety of inquiry skills. This book is intended to increase the probability that novice researchers will develop a realistic and positive attitude toward the practice of research.

Chapter Three

Humanistic Historical Research

Robert A. Carlson

In its commitment to encouraging change, the field of adult education tends to be oriented, in its research, toward present and future. The backward look may seem irrelevant or, at times, even subversive. Indeed, a philosophical or humanistic history of an adult educator's life, past activities, thinking, or organization often challenges assumptions on which the profession is based. The historical study may even question the right of adult educators to attempt to control or change their fellow man. This is the great strength of humanistic history. Because of its potential for challenging basic assumptions, this type of research may offer a unique opportunity to those involved in the study of adult education.

Intent and Approach

Anyone responding to the challenge of humanistic historical research should recognize his concomitant responsibilities for careful investigation and for high-quality literary scholarship. The writing of humanistic history requires not only analytical skills but also the talent and mind set of the playwright. To write history is a two-part endeavor. Historians present a reasoned argument regarding the past, based on evidence and their own values. They must also make the presentation an exciting and literate narrative. Historians, like playwrights (Baritz, 1962), ring up the curtain on the period they choose. They select the lead characters and the bit players. They develop the plot by selecting and arranging the facts. Through the narrative, they illuminate the idea, issue, or thesis related to some topic. And they bring the curtain down when they choose. The writing of high-quality historical research, then, requires that the analytically minded investigator also become adept at writing the narrativ'

Another requirement faces the historian: the need for interpretative creativity within the limits of what happened in the past. Reality disciplines the playwright-historian. He cannot make up people and events out of whole cloth. At the same time, the historian cannot simply chronicle this person and that event, string them together, and have a worthwhile history. Interpretation is essential to a historical study and is at once the most important and most difficult skill to master. Historians interpret the past by sifting through the available relevant evidence and by mixing this information with their own values and philosophy. Through this sometimes agonizing process, they create or discover patterns in the thinking, action, motivation, and relationships that occurred in the past. Disciplined only by reality and their own common sense, historians tease out, dream up, and spin out their interpretation of why the events they are describing have occurred.

Each historian thus writes a personal explanation of the past. The significance and meaning accorded to the facts of history are "necessarily a result of the historian's own conception of himself, his craft, and the motivations of men" (Baritz, 1962, p. 340). The historian's values influence his decisions on what data he incorporates and emphasizes in his writing and the interpretation he makes of those data. Each researcher makes these decisions informally from day to day as he works through his original source material. He does not know the precise direction to be taken until he has studied much of the documentation and is ready to prepare an outline for writing. History, then, is essentially a personal, individual effort to make sense of what has happened at some point in the past.

Steps in the Process

If one is interested in developing a research topic related to the history of adult education, a logical starting point is an interest in some adult education institution, a practitioner or theorist of the field, a particular program or activity, or an idea or concept now or once prevalent in the field. A preliminary check of secondary sources and some informal inquiries of individuals who might be helpful in the research will show whether the study is feasible. The next move is to determine what primary sources will be available, such as correspondence, speeches, articles, and similar material. It is particularly gratifying when those in control of such sources make them available to researchers. If not, the research process is more difficult but still not impossible. A lack of cooperation by those to be studied, for example, is unfortunate, but that should not stop research. In such cases the historian has to rely on other available evidence and do a great deal of inferring from secondary sources. Such history may not be perfect, but it may help open doors for later efforts.

The next step usually is to develop a succinct research proposal or plan that shows the focus of the study. Such a plan, in its early stages, should delineate the general topic, pose some of the questions to be addressed in the study, indicate its limits, and note prospective primary and secondary sources. Eventually, and this may be well along in the process, the historian should update the research proposal to indicate the overall thesis to be argued and to provide an outline that shows how each chapter fits into the pattern of support being built for the thesis.

This type of proposal can help to preserve the humanistic nature of history, avoiding strangulation among the weeds of social science methodology. The historian must be allowed to develop his interpretation and thesis naturally as he works through the source material, building this aspect into his proposal only when he is ready to prepare an outline for the writing of the study. The proposal for a historical study seldom requires an extensive description of methods and should judiciously refrain from stating hypotheses, locking into a social science theory, or articulating the study in the form of a problem. Historical research is not intended for solving problems or for predicting or controlling human action. The intent is to explore issues related to man and his relationships. It is the belief of many historians that man is far too complex and spiritual a creation to be reduced to a problem. Thus, historical research is not a discipline with which to solve problems but a means of exploring the mystery that is man.

Following the development of an acceptable preliminary proposal (one that probably lacks an explicit thesis or chapter outline), the researcher begins a direct involvement with the sources. Some research methods call for certain techniques or a standardized approach to dealing with sources. Historical research discipline, however, urges the investigator to adopt a consistent philosophy of life and to let his research reflect that philosophy. To think of history as a technique is likely to demean it, to reduce it to just another method of snooping into people's lives in an effort to control those lives. Historians, therefore, have never concocted a special language, a consistent theoretical system, or uniform criteria for evaluating their performance.

The historian is not a totally free spirit, though; there are some research requirements. If an investigator engages in historical research, he has to develop ways of dealing intelligently with sources. Obviously, it is necessary to criticize sources for their authenticity or trustworthiness (Carr, 1965, Gottschalk, 1950). Conclusions, theses, and interpretations developed from the data should stand the tests of logic, and the footnoting of sources should enable critics to check accuracy. A bibliography or bibliographical essay is required. So is a table of contents and usually an abstract.

The historian has to deal with and record relevant information from a variety of sources. This activity likely will include archival research, the use of other library resources, interviewing, and note-taking. Does this mean that the historian should take courses in interviewing, note-taking, research methods, and library science? Not necessarily. Such courses may be helpful, but it should be remembered that in history, taking notes, conducting interviews, and the like are very individual undertakings. Though some helpful guidelines are available on these matters, the most important guides to the humanistic historian are to maintain skepticism and common sense.

While working with his sources, the historian begins to develop in his own mind the story he will tell. He begins to look for issues of import that he can fashion into his story. He determines what it is he wants his story to accomplish. He begins to draw out of himself an explanation or interpretation of why the story happened in the way he recounts it. Then he performs the most difficult early requirement: he struggles to develop a thesis or argument around which he will evolve his story.

Theses can range from the simple to the intricate. Several excellent historical studies related to adult education will serve to exemplify what I mean by the term *thesis*. McGinnis (1972) told a story in which he argued that failure was the likely outcome when an adult educator entered a foreign culture to help people develop along lines of interest to that outsider. The failure, McGinnis argued, was devoutly to be wished. He added, however, that such an experience may produce some ancillary results that can justify the otherwise fruitless helping enterprise. The thesis of Dolan (1972) was far less complex. He argued simply that playwright Sean O'Casey was an adult educator who used the theatre as his classroom. Dolan supported his thesis by examining the changing content and process of the playwright's life work. Collins (1972) incisively stated his thesis at the outset: he denied the assumption current in adult education that the founders of mechanics' institutes sought to promote working-class aims. Collins claimed the founders wanted to indoctrinate workers in middle-class values as a bulwark against the furtherance of the political notions of lower-class radicals. Making a strong case for this thesis, he effectively called into question the interpretations of such historians of the field as Thomas Kelly, E. A. Corbett, and Malcolm Knowles. Interpretation and thesis, of course, are intimately connected, often blending into each other, as they did in the Collins study.

Two other studies, like those of McGinnis, Dolan, and Collins, illustrate excellence in the humanistic historical research genre. One is Taylor's study (1965) of recent English history. Though Taylor's book is lengthy and not directly related to the study of adult education, it is an excellent history and an example to consider when doing history on a topic in adult education. The other deals specifically with adult education. It is a seventeen-page article by Weinberg (1968) about adult educators in the World War II Office of War Information (OWI) in the United States. Weinberg, a history instructor in New Jersey, humanized the bureaucracy by describing a writers' quarrel in the OWI. These studies typify a kind of research desperately needed in the field to balance the social science emphasis so prevalent in adult education.

None of the historians thus far cited related his work to any theory. Each was telling a story and illuminating issues. They were not seeking to test or add data to sociological or psychological theory. They wrote history that could be characterized as "unrepentantly and blatantly untheoretical" (Briggs, 1966, p. 195). Any of these historians, however, could easily have allowed his study to be subverted to some existing theory. Collins (1969), for example, could have been trapped into turning his history into an "involvement" or "participation" study, showing how the clientele's background influenced the development of an institution. To take advantage of the full opportunity offered by humanistic historical research, however, the writers had to decide that they were applying history, not social science theory, to the study of adult education.

Historians of adult education are wise to eschew theoretical frameworks for their studies, relying instead on the creation of historical context. They should read extensively about the times to which the topic related. To understand the topic, writers need to know the milieu of the person, institution, activity, or idea being studied. Before and while working the sources, historians should be reading for this type of context. Context is essential to history. Unless the research is fleshed out with some contextual background, the adult education story may float like a disabled spaceship or a disembodied spirit. Context will give the story contact with life, with reality. One does not write about intramural disputes within the Thailand office of an international adult education organization, for example, without bringing in the military dictatorship, American influence, and insurgency in the countryside. It is not a theoretical framework, then, but a historical context that is required of a historical study.

Writing Style and Format

In writing history, one certainly needs balanced judgment, but one ought not to clutch at that wet noodle called objectivity. After making a judgment, historians write in support of that judgment. They take a position and argue it with reasoned passion. In their writing, they marshal the facts to prove their case. They must avoid the extremes of special pleading on one hand and letting the facts speak for themselves on the other. If there is evidence contrary to that being emphasized, they should indicate it briefly and explain why they deemphasized or rejected it in building the case. The historian must not try to hide contrary evidence. At the same time, he cannot rely on the premise that facts can speak for themselves. They cannot speak for themselves. The historian's job is to breathe life and meaning into them.

Some especially effective ways exist for breathing life into the narrative. Good literature requires intelligent organization and a sensitivity to writing style. For example, it is desirable to develop an outline before starting to write. Without some sort of working outline, organization is difficult. The outline will provide tentative chapter headings and will determine when and where the historian presents the various scenes of his story. (This is the outline that becomes a part of the overall proposal for the study.)

Most histories begin with an introductory chapter that supplies the reader with both a road map and an interest in making the trip. The first chapter likely will establish the historical context and introduce the topic. It may also state the thesis to be argued and, perhaps, some of the critical issues that will be at stake in the course of the narrative. The historian then uses each chapter to carry the story along, enticing the reader on to the next chapter until the final chapter is reached. The last chapter in a historical work on adult education will not provide recommended solutions to present problems. If the historian wishes, he may suggest briefly and tentatively some analogy or relationship the story may have to the present. More typically, the final chapter will summarize briefly both the story and the interpretation. It will undoubtedly restate the thesis. It should not be mere repetition, however. It should either carry the story a bit further or explicate the interpretation in a new and exciting way. A bibliography or bibliographical essay should complete the presentation.

The historian must beware of didacticism as he unfolds his story. Too much analysis will render a history cold and lifeless. Too little analysis may leave the story pointless. Drama and analysis must be combined judiciously, with the action carrying as much of the explanation as possible. For example, Dolan could have stated didactically that the main character of his study would be Sean O'Casey, the Irish playwright. He chose, rather, to introduce O'Casey more dramatically: "The gaunt, slightly stooped figure stood hesitantly before the footlights, the peak of his cloth cap pulled down to shield his weak eyes from the harsh glare of the lights. He wore a scarf round his neck, an old trenchcoat, thick working-men's trousers, and the heavy hob-nailed boots of a labourer. The curtain had just fallen on *The Shadow of a Gunman* in the Abbey Theatre in Dublin. It was April, 1923. Sean O'Casey, flushed with the triumph of his first success, peered out at the wildly enthusiastic audience. Another great dramatist had arrived to join the ranks of distinguished Irish writers" (1972, p. 7).

The first paragraph of each chapter can be to that chapter what the introduction is to the total study. Each chapter can begin with a brief introductory paragraph showing where this particular chapter is going and how it fits into the total thesis. The concluding paragraph of each chapter might sum it up and lead the reader in some tantalizing manner on to the next. To avoid dullness, such an approach would require some subtlety and variation. A similar approach has application from paragraph to paragraph through each chapter. Each paragraph can open with a topic sentence that sets the stage for what is to come in the paragraph. Like the last paragraph in a chapter, the last sentence in each paragraph can conclude by briefly summarizing the major point of the paragraph and giving a transition to the next paragraph. This approach is one way to keep from meandering among a number of thoughts in one paragraph and from burying something important within a paragraph, away from the reader's view.

The historian must find his own way of taking charge of the data he has gathered. There is no reason, for example, to be locked into telling a story chronologically. The historian sometimes utilizes materials dated much earlier than the main events in order to develop the motivations for later actions by the characters in the story. He can use flashbacks and other such methods of the playwright. But whatever approaches he may use, it is essential that the historian avoid letting the data control him; he must control the data.

Good literary style in history helps to personalize, humanize, and communicate (Strunk and White, 1965). The writer may sometimes be tempted to seek clarity by dividing the manuscript in some mechanistic way that gives up the attempt at literary style and subtlety. For the sake of the human beings in the story and those reading the story, and perhaps for the sake of his own soul and for the soul that still exists within historical scholarship, the humanistic historian seeks subtlety and sensitivity, as well as clarity. The effective application of history to the study of adult education requires more than clear analysis. It demands good literary style.

An Alternative Way

This chapter has presented a philosophical essay on the writing of humanistic history in adult education. It is, of course, one person's opinion. This is not to demean what has been written. All scholarship, including the most rigorous scientific analysis, comes down to one person's opinion in the end. Whether the opinion is accepted or rejected depends on the cogency of the argument and the skill of the writer. It must be noted that this chapter has championed humanistic history. Social science history is a different genre, based on research patterns discussed in other chapters of this publication. Although the chapter professes humanistic history, its success should not be judged by counting the number of feet of adult education students and practitioners observed newly marching to the drumbeat of humanistic historical research. It should be judged, rather, by how well it shows professionals in the field an alternative way of thinking about research in adult education.

Chapter Four

◆◆◆◆◆◆◆◆◆◆◆◆◆◆◆◆◆◆◆◆◆◆◆
◆◆◆◆◆◆◆◆◆◆◆◆◆◆◆◆◆◆◆◆◆

Survey Research

◆◆◆◆◆◆◆◆◆◆◆◆◆◆◆◆◆◆◆◆◆◆◆
◆◆◆◆◆◆◆◆◆◆◆◆◆◆◆◆◆◆◆◆◆

Gary Dickinson
Adrian Blunt

Much of the substantive knowledge in the emerging discipline of adult education has been acquired in the past twenty years and has been concerned with the extent and nature of adult education as a field of social practice. An inevitable consequence of this emphasis has been the predominance of survey methods over other research methods. The purposes of this chapter are to describe the role of the survey method in adult education research, to identify its strengths and weaknesses, and to discuss the flow of activities together with problems typically encountered in planning and conducting surveys.

The first major survey in adult education was conducted in England in 1851 by Hudson, who felt it important that the public "be placed in possession of such facts as can be collected, to afford a just estimate of the nature and extent of the efforts which have been made, in behalf of adult education, and the effects it has produced" (Hudson, 1969, p. *v*). Accurate description remains a paramount goal in adult education research. Typical subjects for surveys include personnel and staffing, adults' learning needs and interests, program activities, and finance. Perhaps no other topic has been studied more extensively with the survey method than has participation in adult education.

Surveys constitute a major portion of both published non-degree research and unpublished degree research. As Dickinson and Rusnell (1971) point out, *Adult Education*, the principal journal of research and theory in the field, published 117 articles on empirical research in the twenty-year period ending in 1970, and of these, 86 percent reported the use of the survey method. Every empirical-research article published during the first five years of the journal was a survey report, as were 65 percent of the articles in the last five-year period studied. Similarly, 72 percent of the doctoral studies listed in *Adult Education Dissertation Abstracts* (DeCrow and Loague, 1970; Grabowski and Loague, 1970) for the years 1963 through 1969 used descriptive methods, which included case studies as well as surveys. The use of such methods showed no tendency to decrease; indeed, the percentage of all dissertations using descriptive methods steadily increased from 67 percent in 1965 to 75 percent in 1969.

The survey method will probably continue to be the major means used. Even basic information about the extent and nature of present practice in adult education is far from complete, and the field is still expanding and changing; so there will be a continuing need to ensure that knowledge keeps pace with changes in practice. Similarly, the orderly development of a discipline of adult education depends on a steady flow of knowledge acquired through survey research. Knowles (1973) described six phases in the development of evolving disciplines of social practice—definition, differentiation, standard-setting, technological refinement, respectability and justification, and understanding the dynamics of the field—and listed the kinds of research that are needed in each. Survey research has a role in each phase, a crucial role in at least three. Thus, the need for surveys will undoubtedly continue in the future, although their dominance may diminish as other research methods become more appropriate for different developmental phases.

Nature and Purpose

The term *survey research* is applied to a type of social-scientific investigation that "studies large and small populations by selecting and studying samples chosen from the populations to discover the relative incidence, distribution, and interrelations of sociological and psychological variables" (Kerlinger, 1973, p. 410). Surveys vary greatly in complexity, sophistication, and cost, ranging from short-term, clerical studies for clarifying an immediate local problem to major national studies attempting to detect significant interrelationships among complex phenomena. In the literature of adult education, these extremes are represented by such studies as an investigation of the learning interests among members of one school board (Stroup, 1960) and a comprehensive survey of participation in adult education in the United States (Johnstone and Rivera, 1965).

In general, surveys in adult education have been conducted to determine the current status of a phenomenon in the field, rather than to probe deeply into causative factors. The usual purpose has been to acquire information for use in making decisions about programs. Such surveys, however, typically have contributed little to the development of adult education theory, as they have been univariate investigations of multivariate phenomena.

Surveys may be classified in several different ways, with descriptive and analytical categories being used most frequently. Descriptive surveys tend to use small samples, measures of central tendency, and percentage distributions of the variables studied. Some descriptive surveys test hypotheses, but they are not generally characterized by sophisticated data analyses. Analytic surveys tend to use large samples, confidence intervals, tests of significance, and multivariate data analyses. Survey designs also may be classified according to an experimental-model typology. At the simplest level, a preexperimental design known as the "one-shot case study" has features such as the collection of observations at one time only, no control over the effects of variables, and no control groups. Sophisticated survey designs may simulate higher levels of experimental design through the use of stratified random sampling, subsampling, multivariate analysis, and panels of respondents.

Surveys may also be classified by the types of variables studied, such as those sociological or psychological in nature, and by the method of obtaining information, such as the personal interview, telephone interview, mail questionnaire, or controlled observation. Reports of surveys published in *Adult Education* over a twenty-year period suggest that the emphasis in the field has been on descriptive, one-shot surveys studying sociological variables through the use of mailed questionnaires (Dickinson and Rusnell, 1971).

Advantages and Disadvantages

Some of the important strengths of survey research are listed below:

1. Surveys can provide a fairly accurate description of a field or a phenomenon within a field at a given time.
2. A great deal of information can be gathered from representatives of a large population, and the information is accurate within sampling error ranges.
3. Successive surveys of the same population or phenomenon can determine trends over a period of time.
4. Surveys assist in identifying areas where other types of research are needed by suggesting hypotheses and lines of inquiry.
5. Surveys may attempt to simulate experimental designs through the use of multivariate data analysis or by comparing the status of two or more groups at two or more times.
6. Surveys present information about specific, definable populations about which generalizations can be made.
7. Measurements and observations are made in the natural setting.

At the same time, survey research has some obvious weaknesses:

1. Surveys concentrate on describing the present without considering the past or the future.
2. Surveys are not usually employed as part of a long-range, global

research plan; it is difficult to relate a single survey to other
surveys in different places or at different times.
3. The information provided by surveys may be useful to administrators but is not very applicable to work with individuals.
4. The reliability and validity of the responses to survey questions
   are difficult to establish, and subjects' failure to respond may
   affect the results.
5. Conducting a survey requires skill in a wide variety of research
   techniques and procedures.
6. Surveys are ponderous in that once a design is established, it is
   difficult to modify.
7. A considerable amount of manpower, time, and money is required to do a survey.
8. The variables are not usually controlled; so there are a large
   number of sources of potential error and bias in survey data.
9. The cooperation of individuals is required, but it may not be
   given by the total sample.

The relatively unsophisticated nature of survey research in
adult education has been inevitable in an emerging discipline which
lacks a tradition of rigorous empirical research. The increasing number of persons who have earned doctorates in adult education is
evidence that the field is beginning to develop a corps of specialists
with interest, training, and experience in research procedures. The
limitations inherent in the survey method are still quite obvious in
much of the research produced in adult education, while the potential strengths, with rare exceptions, have not been fully realized.

The full gamut of complexity and sophistication that is
possible in survey research can be observed in the body of studies
related to participation in adult education; hence, a perusal of
a selection of such studies would be valuable for those aspiring to
conduct a survey. Relatively few studies have used complex research designs, and these are usually beyond the abilities and
resources of a single researcher. Surveys of participation within a
community or an institution are more feasible for the individual.
Until recently, participation surveys generally employed simple
forms of data analysis that rarely extended beyond frequency and
percentage distributions, but some researchers are using more

sophisticated types of statistical analyses to identify specific phenomena related to participation in adult education (Boshier, 1971; Dickinson, 1971; Kronus, 1973; Litchfield, 1965).

Elements of Survey Design

Designing a survey requires the selection of specific procedures and techniques from a wide range of options. Thus the selection process is a complex matter requiring considerable judgment, as there is no single design that is appropriate for every survey. Our intent here is to outline briefly the basic components of survey design and to identify some difficulties the researcher might encounter. Although these elements may not be chronologically discrete or considered in isolation, the major phases in survey design constitute a sequence which conforms to general models of educational research.

The Problem. Obviously, a first step is to choose and define the problem to be investigated. The initial search for a researchable problem may be stimulated by personal experience working in the field, by informal discussions with other researchers, and by critically reading the general literature and previous research in adult education. Although the selection of a specific problem is primarily the responsibility of the researcher, the decision is often influenced by other researchers, agencies offering adult education programs, and funding organizations. The problem selected should be interesting to the investigator personally as well as to others in the field, should promise to contribute to the body of knowledge in adult education, should be investigatable with existing survey methods, and should promise to produce benefits worth the cost, time, and effort required. To meet these criteria, researchers cannot choose a problem until they have acquired experience in the field, have read widely in the literature, and have gained considerable knowledge about research methods and techniques so that they can judge whether a particular problem can be resolved with available resources and whether the problem is worth resolving. A negative answer in either case should result in the rejection of a problem.

A precise and explicit statement of the problem must be developed in order to define and limit the scope of the survey.

Early drafts of a problem statement may tend to be vague and general, but subsequent drafts should sharpen it. Refinement will assist researchers in focusing their efforts and will enable them to communicate the problem accurately to others who may be involved in the research. An imprecise statement of a problem can lead the researcher to develop unrealistic expectations for a study and may result in such a diffusion of energy that the original purpose of the study is forgotten.

The Hypotheses. Once the research problem is clearly defined, it must be presented so that data can be collected and analyzed to resolve the problem. The problem may be posed as a question or several questions that could be answered by collecting descriptive data or as hypotheses to be tested with survey data and accepted or rejected at a predetermined level of statistical significance. In a survey of dropouts from night-school courses, for example, the problem might be phrased as the question What is the average age of night school dropouts compared with those who do not drop out? A hypothesis dealing with the same topic might be this: Those who drop out will have a lower average age than those who do not drop out.

The latter statement is considered a research hypothesis because it is a proposition supported by existing knowledge which describes an expected relationship between two variables. Such hypotheses give direction and precision to the development of a survey design and help to prevent the collection of extraneous data. At the appropriate time during data analysis, the research hypotheses may be restated as null hypotheses for statistical testing.

The most suitable point in a survey to formulate research hypotheses varies with the nature of the problem and the extent of existing knowledge about it. A survey may begin with precise hypotheses derived from previous research, or if previous research is lacking, it may begin with a series of questions and conclude with hypotheses developed from the data collected.

Every survey should build on the findings and methods of previous surveys and serve as a basis for future research. One of the first steps in designing a survey, therefore, is to establish links with existing research and theory so that a single survey is not conducted in isolation. A review and analysis of existing research and theory will help the researcher develop a perspective for the survey, establish its unique contribution to the discipline of adult education, and avoid any unwarranted replication of previous research.

The construction of an appropriate theoretical framework involves the identification, or creation, of relevant concepts and constructs which are generalizations of particular behaviors or conditions that can be observed and measured. The expected relationships among these concepts are stated as research hypotheses. In order to test those relationships, the concepts and constructs must be defined operationally so that empirical observations may be carried out and relevant data accumulated.

The Population and Sample. Another element is defining the population and selecting the sample. The population for a survey consists of the total number of units under consideration in the research problem. Because survey research attempts to estimate values in and make generalizations to given populations, Kish (1965) believes the relevant population must be specified exactly: its characteristics, the units to be studied, its geographic area, and the period in which it will be studied.

Selecting an adequate sample from a specified population is crucial to a successful survey; yet that phase is often poorly handled. Quite frequently, a sample is selected that does not adequately represent the population under study or is not large enough to yield precise analytical results. These inadequacies in sample designs are usually attributed to limitations of money or time. The dangers in compromising the sample size because of cost and time factors are that the sample may be biased and the results may not be sufficiently precise to enable the hypotheses to be tested. Furthermore, the accuracy of survey results is not determined by the number or proportion of population elements included in the sample. Rather, accuracy depends on the size of the sample itself; thus the determination of size should be governed by the desired precision of the survey results, the number of variables being investigated, and the distribution of those variables in the population. In general, descriptive surveys use smaller samples than do analytic surveys, as breakdowns of the sample into subsamples for purposes of multivariate analysis are not required.

A summary of the characteristics as well as the advantages

and disadvantages of different types of sampling plans may be
found in many basic research books. However, Selltiz and others
(1959) suggest that any sampling design under consideration
should be evaluated according to the following criteria:

1. Goal orientation. The survey research objectives must be met at
   all levels by the sample design.
2. Representativeness. The sample should accurately represent the
   population from which it is drawn.
3. Measurability. The sample design must allow estimates of sampling variability and statistical tests to be computed.
4. Practicality. The sample design must translate theoretical sampling models into clear, simple, practical, and complete instructions for the conduct of the survey.
5. Sampling Procedure. The means of drawing the sample should
   be in strict accordance with sampling theory.
6. Economy. The sample design should allow the survey objectives
   to be achieved at minimum cost.

The Instrument. Another important element of survey research is the construction of the data-collection instrument, whose
function is to gather the data required to resolve the research
problem. Most surveys use either an interview schedule or a mailed
questionnaire, each having a number of advantages and disadvantages. The selection of an appropriate instrument should be
guided by the nature of the research problem, the size and distribution of the sample, the research hypotheses, and the available
time, money, and supportive services. The instrument chosen should
be evaluated, suggest Hill and Kerber (1967), with respect to its
reliability, validity, objectivity, and discriminatory power. The
instrument should produce consistent results over repeated trials,
measure what it is designed to measure, provide data that can be
consistently evaluated and interpreted by other investigators, and
differentiate among respondents to provide the variation required
for statistical analysis. Wherever possible, existing instruments with
known reliability and validity should be selected. If suitable scales
or indexes are not available, they must be constructed following

recognized scaling procedures, such as those developed by Likert, Thurstone, Guttman, and others (Fishbein, 1967).

The accuracy of the data collected in any survey depends on the willingness and ability of the respondents to provide the desired information, and this is influenced in part by the clarity of the instructions and items included in the instrument. The researcher should minimize the probability of error due to carelessness, ignorance, misunderstanding, or deception on the part of respondents in order to avoid jeopardizing the validity of the instrument. A pretest of the instrument will enable the researcher to assess the frequency of errors, and the accuracy of the data provided should be verified if possible through independent sources. Follow-up interviews can verify the reliability of responses to a mailed questionnaire. And teaching interviewers how to conduct interviews and to record and code verbal information can increase the objectivity and accuracy of data collected on interview schedules.

Survey instruments must be developed with the proposed data analysis in mind so that appropriate levels of measurement are used. Four such levels are almost universally recognized in the social sciences: nominal, ordinal, interval, and ratio. These levels are described in almost every contemporary statistics textbook, but there is still some debate about which statistical tests are appropriate for each level of measurement. In general, it is advisable to collect data using the highest possible level of measurement, because translation to a lower level may be done after the data are collected, but conversion to a higher level may not. Whatever the levels of measurement selected, the instrument should be precoded to minimize time and error in data processing after the data are gathered.

The Final Steps. When the survey instrument is judged to be complete, a pilot study of a small sample of respondents will indicate the probable nonresponse rate, the variability of the responses to specific items, the suitability of the questions, the adequacy of the instructions provided, the appropriateness of the format and sequence of questions, the adequacy of the coding plan, and the time and cost of data collection. The experience gained in a pilot study will usually result in changes in the instruments that will improve the quality of the data collected by the full survey and reduce the costs. Once the pilot study has been completed, the overall survey design should be reviewed and evaluated following a routine such as that suggested in the Research Profiling Flow Chart (Gephart and Bartos, 1969).

Before administering the survey instrument, the researcher should develop a plan for the data analysis to indicate how each variable will be used. The variables to be used in hypothesis testing should be identified with their respective hypotheses, while other variables thought to be useful for explanatory purposes in secondary analyses should be scrutinized closely and discarded if their utility is not readily apparent. In some cases, hypotheses may be revised to include such additional variables. The appropriate statistical tests should be selected and the levels of measurement assessed to ensure that the assumptions underlying the tests are met by the format of the data to be collected. Although texts can help the researcher choose the right statistical tests, guides using a "decision tree" approach, such as the one published by the Survey Research Center at the University of Michigan (Andrews and others, n.d.), provide a systematic means of selecting appropriate tests. Tests of significance are used frequently in survey research in adult education, whereas confidence intervals are rarely used; however, this practice is not supported by some statisticians, who contend that data presented in terms of confidence intervals are often more meaningful than those presented with tests of significance (Kish, 1959; Stanley, 1966). In addition to selecting the most suitable statistical tests, the researcher should prepare specimen tables to indicate the format and content of the data to be presented in the survey report.

If the analysis plan is sufficiently detailed, hypothesis testing becomes a routine procedure. The analysis, however, should extend beyond the routine testing of hypotheses to probe, as Rosenberg (1968) suggests, the validity of alternative explanations. The logical probing of data can lead the researcher to identify new explanatory variables and formulate new hypotheses which must be tested in subsequent studies. The process of elaboration involving the analysis of subgroups within a sample is also a useful way of investigating relationships among survey data (Lazarsfeld and others, 1972;

Rosenberg, 1968). Although the researcher cannot make detailed plans in advance for all secondary types of data analysis, he should give some general consideration to the procedures that will be followed in order to avoid the everything-against-everything approach that is facilitated by the availability of a computer. The purpose of data analysis is not to produce as many statistically significant results as possible, but rather to evaluate the magnitude and meaning of differences to identify those that are of substantive significance.

A description of all the procedures and potential problems related to carrying out a survey in adult education from the design stage to completion is beyond the scope of this chapter. But, in brief, the major phases in implementing the survey design consist of collecting and processing the data, analyzing the data, and preparing the survey report. Each of these phases requires a degree of sophistication and skill in making appropriate decisions to ensure that the survey design is followed. The study of a variety of available works on research and actual experience in carrying out well-designed survey projects will contribute to the building of such abilities.

Problems of Survey Research

The discipline of adult education has acquired much of its substantive content by borrowing and reformulating knowledge from other disciplines, and the knowledge so acquired is expanding at an increasing rate. However, there has not been a concurrent borrowing and reformulation of knowledge pertaining to the research methods developed in other disciplines; survey research in education generally has been characterized as backward and unsophisticated (Cornell and McLoore, 1963; Trow, 1967).

One reason, unfortunately, is that the training in research currently received by adult educators does not do much to help them develop the skills required to conduct the kinds of survey research that might advance the discipline the most at the present time. Instead of giving preparation related to research design and analysis strategies and the logic of survey research, such training tends to emphasize either the derivation of statistics and precision in experimental design or the technology of conducting surveys. These emphases contribute, for example, to the widespread use of hypothesis testing as opposed to the use of confidence intervals. As a consequence, adult educators often search for statistical rather than substantive significance. The integration of empirical and theoretical elements found in other social sciences, such as sociology, which are more advanced than education with respect to the state of survey research, may be more appropriate to the needs of adult education.

The reliability and validity of survey research in adult education needs to be increased by exerting greater control over the sources of error. As Deming (1970) suggests, the factors contributing to error are many, but their effects can be minimized through such steps as adhering rigorously to sampling procedures; determining acceptable levels of sampling error; using only reliable, pretested instruments; increasing accuracy in recording, processing, and reporting data; and recognizing the assumptions underlying the use of statistical tests and data manipulation. The validity of survey research in adult education could also be increased considerably through wider use of the "triangulation of methodologies" process described by Denzin (1970). In the "within-method" approach to triangulation, a single research method, such as the survey, uses several scales to measure the same phenomenon, while a "between-methods" approach uses several research methods to collect data about the same phenomenon. Research hypotheses tested with data from a series of complementary investigations or measures can attain results of higher validity than those attainable in a study using a single method or instrument.

Survey research in adult education tends to lack rigor and sophistication. For the most part, surveys have been conducted by individuals within a brief time, and the primary goal has been to complete graduate degree requirements rather than to make a significant contribution to the emerging discipline of adult education. Many important problems in the field remain to be resolved, but individuals with little time and money cannot be expected to resolve them. Sophisticated and potentially valuable research designs require a long-term commitment of resources and personnel and can be used only if teams of researchers can be formed and supported so that the complex tasks of survey research may be undertaken cooperatively.

Chapter Five

Field Research
and Grounded Theory

Gordon G. Darkenwald

This chapter deals with an approach to social research that is little known outside sociology and that departs sharply from the logico-deductive paradigm of experimental science long dominant in educational inquiry. Not only is grounded theory unconventional and unfamiliar, but its methods have yet to be clearly codified and continue to be subject to varying interpretations. Despite these difficulties, grounded theory offers the adult education researcher a new and promising alternative to traditional ways of conceptualizing and conducting empirical studies.

The term *grounded theory* gained currency with the publication of Glaser and Strauss's seminal book, *The Discovery of Grounded Theory* (1967), which sets forth the scientific rationale and the data-collection and analysis techniques for this distinctive style of inquiry. Essentially, grounded theory is an inductive approach to research that focuses on social interaction and relies heavily on data from interviews and observations to build theory grounded in the data rather than to test theory or simply describe empirical phenomena. It is closely related to the sociological and anthropological fieldwork traditions exemplified by such familiar works as *Street Corner Society* (Whyte, 1941) and *Tally's Corner* (Liebow, 1967). Perhaps the major distinction between grounded theory and traditional field work is that grounded theory is less concerned with detailed description and holistic interpretation than with generalized explanations of the social phenomena under study. To facilitate the development of theoretical generalizations, grounded-theory researchers rely heavily on comparative analysis, whereas many social scientists who use field methods confine their research to the intensive study of a single group, tribe, organization, or other social collectivity.

This chapter is addressed primarily to researchers who may be interested in, but unfamiliar with, the grounded-theory approach. Consequently, I have tried to keep the discussion basic and practical. The following pages provide a broad view of the nature of grounded theory and its uses, describe the elements of data collection and analysis, and give examples of the application of grounded-theory methods to research in adult education. Before discussing grounded theory in more detail, however, I must note a few caveats.

First of all, grounded-theory research is probably more difficult than the typical descriptive or experimental study. Researchers need to master its logic and techniques, just as they need to master the intricacies of experimental design, measurement, and statistical analysis to undertake more traditional investigations. But there are special problems with grounded theory. Most vexing is the lack of easily understood, codified rules for the collection and analysis of qualitative data and the construction of theory. As in anthropological or historical research, there is more than a little art involved in doing a grounded-theory study. The interested researcher, furthermore, is not likely to find training opportunities or a course in grounded-theory methods, although most universities do offer courses in fieldwork techniques that would be very helpful. For the most part, however, researchers are left to their own devices. Consequently, a good deal of independent reading, as well as small-scale trial efforts in the field, are essential before a major grounded-theory investigation is launched. Another practical consideration is the amount of effort normally required. Much time must be spent in the field collecting data, which must be transcribed and painstakingly analyzed; and writing reports of grounded-theory research tends to be more exacting than reporting the results of conventional research. The caveats aside, grounded-theory research can be rewarding both personally and professionally. Getting out of the library or computer center and into the world of educational practice can be an exhilarating and enlightening experience.

Nature of Grounded Theory

Much important material, particularly concerning the scientific logic and methodology of grounded theory, is necessarily omitted from this chapter. As I said, the basic reference is Glaser and Strauss (1967); the first five chapters bear rereading several times. Mezirow (1971) has written a provocative article criticizing the assumptions of traditional social science research and outlining the potential of grounded-theory studies for upgrading professional practice in adult education. Grounded theory is usually identified with the sociological tradition of symbolic interactionism that has its epistemological roots in the work of G. H. Mead and John Dewey. The standard work on symbolic interactionism is by Blumer (1969). A critique of symbolic interactionism and grounded theory has been published in the *American Sociological Review* (Huber, 1973). For a comprehensive, step-by-step treatment of fieldwork techniques and the analysis of qualitative data, the researcher should consult Schatzman and Strauss (1973). This work is invaluable for any researcher preparing to undertake a grounded-theory study. Several methodology texts include material on fieldwork methods, notably Adams and Preiss (1960), Filstead (1970), Hammond (1964), and McCall and Simmons (1969). An orthodox example of a grounded-theory study is Glaser and Strauss's *Awareness of Dying*

(1965). For examples of doctoral dissertations in adult education that have used grounded-theory techniques, see Beder (1972), Israeli (1973), and MacNeil (1970).

A typical definition of theory is given by Kerlinger: "A theory is a set of interrelated constructs (concepts), definitions, and propositions that present a systematic view of phenomena by specifying relations among variables, with the purpose of explaining and predicting the phenomena" (1973, p. 9). Glaser and Strauss accept this definition, but go beyond it in their contention that good theory should not only explain and predict but also be useful. In their view, the functions of theory are these: "(1) to enable prediction and explanation of behavior; (2) to be useful in theoretical advance; (3) to be useful in practical applications—prediction and explanation should be able to give the practitioner understanding and some control of situations; (4) to provide a perspective on behavior—a stance to be taken toward data; and (5) to guide and provide a style for research on particular areas of behavior" (1967, p. 3).

Assuming that theory should provide understanding and some control of real-life situations, what is the best way to develop it? Glaser and Strauss argue persuasively that theory should be inductively generated through the systematic analysis of empirical data. Furthermore, in their view, the key to successful theory generation is the use of the general comparative method. That is, in order to discover the basic conceptual elements of theory, one must systematically compare similar, and sometimes dissimilar, events or situations. Only in this way can theory be progressively built up so that it is generally applicable to the social behavior under study. Much theory in the social sciences, in contrast, is based not on careful analysis of empirical data but rather on speculation and logical deduction from sometimes dubious a priori assumptions. Such theory is often so abstract that its relationship to the real world is barely discernible, and putting concepts into operation to test the theory is virtually impossible. Theory that fits the world that human beings inhabit and that has endured (for example, Weber on bureaucracy, Durkheim on suicide, and Piaget on child development) has invariably been grounded in empirical inquiry.

Data for the generation of grounded theory can come from any source, including documents and records and previous research. In most cases, however, the bulk of the data is obtained through participant observation, a fieldwork strategy in which the researcher gets to know the situation and the people involved at first hand and collects data largely through careful observation of behavior and informal interviewing.

The conceptual elements (constructs) of grounded theory are referred to as categories and properties. A category is a basic theoretical concept that enables the researcher to explain and predict behavior. A property is a conceptual element of a category that serves to define or elaborate the meaning of the category. Thus, categories and their properties are closely related. Grounded theory also consists of propositions or hypotheses that specify the relationships among categories. A fully developed set of categories, definitions, and propositions, integrated in an analytical scheme, comprises the core of the grounded theory. These basic elements of theory are discussed and illustrated in greater detail in subsequent pages. But it might be noted here that these fundamental elements of grounded theory are the same as those of any other kind of theory. What is different is the way in which grounded theory is generated.

Grounded theory can be either formal or substantive. Substantive theory deals with a particular limited domain of inquiry, such as preschool programs, emergency-room care, or university extension services. A substantive theory is close to the real-world situation. A formal theory, in contrast, deals with a general domain of social science, such as socialization or formal organization, and is necessarily more general and conceptually abstract. The construction of formal theory is the proper concern of academic social scientists, whereas the construction of substantive theory is, or should be, a concern of researchers in applied professional fields such as adult education.

Grounded theory is seldom presented as a tightly knit set of interrelated categories, definitions, and propositions. Rather, the theory is discursively developed in narrative form as categories, and their relationships are defined, elaborated, and illustrated by the data (for example, incidents from field reports) used to generate

them. Thus, the most useful and natural form for the presentation
of a grounded-theory analysis is a running discussion that permits
full elaboration of the situation or problem under study.

It may be useful at this point to highlight briefly some
similarities and differences between grounded theory and other
empirical research methods and styles. A fundamental characteristic
of grounded-theory research is that it seeks explanations. Experimental or quasi-experimental research, in contrast, is concerned
mainly with verifying hypotheses—with testing rather than discovering theory. Of course, grounded-theory researchers are also concerned with verification in that they require evidence to establish
the existence of their categories and the validity of their propositions.
But in grounded-theory studies, verification is subordinated to discovery, while the reverse is true in experimental investigations.
Surveys, though sometimes used in quasi-experimental designs, are
often employed for descriptive purposes. Statistical sampling procedures are used in order to ascertain within a specified margin of
error the distribution of variables in a population. Grounded-theory
researchers are also interested in description, particularly of social
processes not amenable to measurement by survey instruments. But
description, like verification, is not the primary objective of
grounded-theory investigation. Quantitative exploratory research,
which often employs powerful statistical techniques such as multiple
regression, resembles grounded theory to the extent that it focuses on
explanation rather than description or verification. Research of this
kind, however, is often problem-oriented and atheoretical. None of
the research approaches mentioned above has as its major concern
the systematic exploration and illumination of social interaction in
real-life settings.

Case studies, including ethnographies, do, however, resemble
grounded theory when the researcher's main intent is to deveolp an
analytical description of human behavior in a naturalistic setting.
As noted previously, the grounded theorist uses the general comparative method to build substantive theory that has general applicability to the particular type of social process or collectivity
under investigation. In contrast, traditional fieldwork tends to focus
on the detailed, holistic analysis of a single case. For generating substantive theory, comparative analysis has obvious advantages over

single case studies because emergent categories and propositions can be elaborated and checked out by collecting data from a variety of comparison groups. This is not to say that when the grounded-theory style of research (that is, one characterized by flexibility, an emphasis on discovery, and an analytical stance toward data) is deftly employed, case studies cannot yield valuable results. An outstanding example is the Clark study (1968) of the Los Angeles school system's adult education program, in which the key category of marginality was formulated and related to such factors as the school system's priorities, securing a clientele, finances, staffing, and facilities. Unfortunately, the typical case study in adult education research lacks this kind of analytical rigor.

The purpose of developing a substantive theory is to shed light on some aspect of human interaction. Consequently, the grounded-theory researcher is interested in studying a particular type of social process or social collectivity (group, organization unit). Glaser and Strauss (1965), for example, studied the hospital care of dying patients. In the field of adult education, there are numerous topics well suited to grounded-theory analysis, such as literacy education in developing countries, program development in university extension, rural community development, and continuing professional education, to mention only a few. It may sound strange to speak of a "theory" of literacy education. Perhaps theory is too grandiose a term to use for such an undertaking. The intent, nonetheless, is not merely to describe but also to explain and permit prediction of human behavior in a carefully delimited context.

Ultimately, the use of grounded theory in applied fields such as adult education is to improve professional practice through gaining a better understanding of it. It seems self-evident that little improvement can be expected without further systematic knowledge concerning what is actually going on in adult education programs. If the subject matter of the field is the process of adult education, then the actual behavior of students, teachers, and administrators and their interpretations of their experience are of central importance for developing theory and upgrading practice.

Iannaccone has put the problem succinctly in an article deploring the present state of research in educational administration: "Despite our achievements to date, the black box of research in educational administration is the school and its work, including that of the administrators. We have tested more hypotheses than we have derived from theory. We have related inputs to outputs. We know more about pupil, teacher, and administrator characteristics and about achievement, responses and community reactions than we know about what people do—how they move and live in schools. Given the present state of the art, we know more about the former classes of variables than we can fruitfully use. Until we understand the school as a world of work and why it is what it is, the development of relevant theory in educational administration will continue to falter" (1973, pp. 62–63).

Data Collection and Analysis

Doing any kind of research well requires experience, and this truism applies with particular force to grounded theory. Although grounded theory has its methods, they are not highly codified, in large part because discovery can never be a mechanical process. The researcher who approaches a grounded-theory study without an appetite for exploration and a tolerance for ambiguity is doomed to frustration from the start.

The techniques of grounded-theory data collection and analysis are described in detail in the first chapters of Glaser and Strauss (1967) and also in somewhat more basic form in Schatzman and Strauss (1973). Much of the material in the former book is likely to be incomprehensible unless one has actually made some attempt to collect and code data. The following pages touch on some of the basic elements of doing grounded-theory research, drawing mostly from Glaser and Strauss, my own experience, and that of my students.

Although it is possible to collect data and later undertake a grounded-theory analysis, it is far more desirable, for reasons that will become evident later, to collect and analyze data simultaneously from the beginning. This involves "theoretical sampling" and continuous coding and analysis. Theoretical sampling is the "process of data collecting for generating theory whereby the analyst jointly collects, codes, and analyzes his data and decides what data to collect next and where to find them, in order to develop his theory as it emerges" (Glaser and Strauss, 1967, p. 45). A statistical sample is drawn in advance of research, but in theoretical sampling the emerging theory dictates where the investigator will go next to collect needed data. For this reason, grounded-theory researchers are never sure at the beginning of a study how many groups or situations they will need to compare. Of course, researchers must start somewhere. Usually, they start by having open-ended interviews with key actors in the situation or by observing some activity. Then comes the difficult task of analyzing the initial data in the research for tentative categories. A category, to reiterate, is a conceptual element in a theory; that is, an analytical concept such as "marginality" that is important in understanding the phenomenon under study.

Normally, investigators begin the search for categories by looking in the data for strategic commonalities and differences. For example, in a study of urban adult basic education (ABE) programs Mezirow, Darkenwald, and Knox (1975) sifted through numerous field reports from participant observers in ABE classrooms. After much tedious work, a number of commonalities and differences in classroom interactions were identified. Teachers' behavior in response to students' failure struck the analysts as surprisingly uniform and at variance with common practice in traditional classrooms. Teachers almost never confronted students with their failure by saying, for example, "No, that's not correct. Does anyone else know the answer?" Instead, the teachers made every effort, in a variety of ingenious ways, to mitigate the students' sense of failure. This category was labeled "failure reduction," and its properties were elaborated. The properties of failure reduction are largely the ways teachers attempt to reduce failure, such as by breaking a problem down into simple, step-by-step components ("working through"), by prompting, and by quickly substituting a new question or assignment.

It takes only a little reflection to see that a category such as failure reduction probably would never be discovered by observing the interaction of students and teachers in only one or two classrooms. Even if an astute analyst identified the category, it would be impossible to be sure of its validity and to fully develop its properties and relationships to other key variables without the aid of theoretical sampling—that is, without looking for additional incidents of failure-reduction behavior in other classrooms to confirm its existence and elaborate its dimensions.

As the analysis progressed, an explanation of failure-reduction behavior began to take form. The numbers game has a pervasive influence on ABE, indeed on most of adult education. Since budgets are largely predicated on the number of students enrolled, it is vital to the organization to recruit and retain as many clients as possible. Teachers are aware of this situation, and they know that they are evaluated in part on how well they hold their students. If attendance falls below a certain level, the teacher may well be out of a job. Consequently, aware that students fear failure, teachers do everything in their power to relieve this threat in the hope of preventing dropouts.

It is an easy step from the elaboration of the category of failure reduction to the formulation of theoretical propositions. For example, the following hypothesis follows logically: Teachers exhibit greater failure-reduction behavior when the organizational need to increase or maintain student enrollment is high. Certain practical implications of the foregoing analysis (necessarily oversimplified here) are also easy to deduce. If one assumes that the sensitivity to students' needs which is characteristic of failure-reduction behavior is desirable, it follows that eliminating the enrollment economy that typifies ABE programs will have certain undesirable consequences. That is, if ABE programs were subsidized in the same manner as elementary schools, it is reasonable to predict that ABE teachers, secure in their jobs, would begin to behave more like traditional schoolteachers and that students would pay the price.

Identifying categories is one of the most difficult tasks in grounded-theory research. Theoretical sensitivity, as Glaser and Strauss (1967, p. 46) point out, is essential, and it is largely acquired by experience. But qualitative analysis is not an esoteric art. The basic idea is to search for commonalities and differences in the data that seem important in understanding what is going on in the situation at hand. Often, the first categories uncovered are too vague or descriptive to provide much explanatory power. Concepts such as trust, authority, or cooperation may suggest themselves; but obviously they are much too general for illuminating social behavior in a particular, substantive context. Analytically potent categories are usually abstracted from the content of the research situation. Failure reduction is an example. In some cases, existing concepts are utilized, provided they fit the data. In the ABE study (Mezirow, Darkenwald, and Knox, 1975), "control" appeared to be an appropriate category to indicate an important dimension of teachers' behavior in ABE classrooms. The meaning of control in the context of ABE was made clear by illustrations from the data and by elaborating its properties, namely the techniques that teachers use to maintain control. As the research unfolds by comparing groups or events to elaborate and test the validity of emergent categories and hypotheses, some of the original categories may be discarded, while others may be reconceptualized to achieve greater specificity and analytical power.

The mechanics of qualitative analysis are relatively straight-forward, and adherence to them can preclude a great deal of trouble. A number should be assigned to each emerging category. Incidents in field reports illustrating the category can then be coded in the margin of the report. Glaser and Strauss (1967, pp. 106–107) suggest that when coding an incident for a particular category, the researcher compare it with other incidents previously coded in the same category. This procedure facilitates the generation of theoretical properties and the elaboration of the category and its relationship to other categories. I have found that McBee key sort cards greatly facilitate analysis and writing. The researcher simply pastes an incident from a field report on the card and punches the number assigned to the category on the edge of the card. It is also important to code and punch for additional information. In the ABE study, each McBee card was punched according to a coding scheme that included categories for staff role (teacher, aide), type of class (basic education, English as a second language), type of facility, and location (city). Once the cards are punched, a simple mechanical procedure allows the researcher to sort out all incidents coded for a particular category or to go even further and sort all incidents for a particular category by staff role, location, and so on.

At various points in the process of analysis, researchers are likely to feel confused, unsure of what to do next, or eager to consolidate their thoughts. It is helpful simply to stop when such a point comes, take time for reflection, and summarize in writing the main elements of the emerging analysis and the logical next steps in data collection. Such periodic summaries of the research situation are extremely valuable for giving direction to the research and building the analysis systematically and cumulatively. Researchers who fail to begin analysis when they start to collect data and who do not take stock of the research situation periodically run a grave risk of being overwhelmed by a mountain of field reports. In one case, a graduate student spent more than a year collecting data without the direction afforded by continuous analysis and theoretical sampling. Two thousand typewritten pages of field notes were assembled, but the researcher was unable to make sense of the data and finally gave up in despair.

A question that invariably arises in doing grounded-theory research is, Where does it end? How does one know when enough data have been collected? The time to stop collecting data for a particular category is when theoretical saturation has been achieved. A category is saturated when continued data collection yields no new information on the properties of the category—the analyst begins to spin wheels. Since categories are identified at various points in the progress of the research, some are saturated before others. It is important, however, that all the categories believed to be of major importance be fully saturated before one terminates data collection and turns to the task of writing.

The problems of writing a grounded-theory research report can be minimized by following closely the data collection and analysis procedures suggested by Glaser and Strauss (1967). When the fieldwork is finished, the researcher should have a set of memos that cumulatively develop the core of the emerging theory. Moreover, theoretical sampling to collect data in conjunction with ongoing analysis naturally leads to a fairly well-integrated set of categories and propositions by the time major categories are saturated. In writing their theories, researchers rely on their research memos and coded field reports. The memos contain the logic of the analysis, that is, the content of the categories and their properties and an exposition of their interrelationships. Normally, major categories provide the basic organizing scheme (or themes) of the research report. Coded data from the field reports (actual incidents, quotations) are used to illustrate categories and their properties. For example, the chapter on classroom dynamics in the study of ABE discussed above was organized around the key process categories of attending (patterns of instructional interaction), failure reduction, and control. The properties of each category (for example, the various techniques of failure reduction) were illustrated by excerpts from field reports. The elements of the substantive theory are developed discursively in the research report as categories and their properties are identified, defined, and illustrated by the data.

Integration with Survey Methods

In many cases, the researcher may not wish to generate a fully developed grounded theory, but rather to use grounded-theory techniques for analytical description or to combine grounded theory with survey research. Case studies, as discussed previously, can sometimes contribute to theory and practice if the researcher takes an analytical stance toward the data and seeks not only to describe but also to explain.

Description is useful when little is known about the topic being investigated and when data of adequate generality can be secured. Certainly, little is known about many important aspects of adult education. To ascertain the state of the art, one needs descriptive information. But it is possible to go beyond simple description to achieve more incisive and generalizable findings. For example, when the aim of an investigation is to develop an analytical description of a type of organization or organizational subunit, field research may be combined with survey techniques. This marriage of methods capitalizes on the strengths of each and can yield far richer results than when only one method or the other is used. Sieber, in fact, contends that the integration of field and survey methods constitutes a new style of research that opens "enormous opportunities...for improving our social research strategies" (1973, p. 1340).

The study of urban ABE programs, discussed previously, attempted to integrate grounded-theory and survey methods to develop an analytical description of urban ABE. Grounded-theory techniques were used when the focus of research was social interaction, as in the case of classroom dynamics and the use of para-professionals. In these parts of the study the research proceeded along the lines described by Glaser and Strauss (1967). However, for other parts of the study it was necessary to obtain reliable descriptive data by surveying teachers and program directors. The surveys yielded a dependable national picture of program characteristics (for example, size, facilities, client populations) and provided reliable descriptive information about teachers and directors that could not be obtained by field methods. The fieldwork, however, greatly aided in the choice and development of survey items which seemed to offer the possibility of clarifying the role of selected variables. The surveys, in turn, were used to test the universality of certain fieldwork findings.

The joint use of field and survey methods, as noted above, enables the researcher to exploit the advantages of both types of data while minimizing their weaknesses. When accurate description is important, or when the focus is on static variables such as organizational size, survey data tend to be most useful. When the emphasis is on human interaction and the development of an analytical framework to explain it, then qualitative data and grounded-theory analysis are required. Where appropriate, the researcher should consider the advantages of combining fieldwork with at least a modest survey.

In conclusion, grounded theory is no panacea to remedy the lack of systematic knowledge that inhibits meaningful efforts to improve professional practice in adult education. Adult educators need to make more effective use of the full range of social-science research strategies available to them and to continue to borrow relevant findings from the social sciences. Moreover, it is not only empirical research that is woefully inadequate. The dearth of good historical and philosophical inquiry also seriously handicaps the development of the field.

Many research problems can only be addressed by using conventional social-science methods. Others require a more flexible heuristic style, particularly when the emphasis is on understanding social interaction in substantive areas of professional practice. It is time for more researchers in adult education to get out in the field and to try to interpret what is happening there. Ultimately, research in education must be grounded in a firm understanding of the realities of practice. Otherwise, as Iannaccone has warned, studies will continue to be produced that are "methodologically bad, theoretically useless, and...focused on trivial problems" (1973, p. 65). For the educational researcher, grounded theory has pitfalls but also exciting possibilities.

Chapter Six

Experimental
Research

Huey B. Long

As adult educators investigate increasingly complex issues, they are likely to use different parts of the descriptive-correlational-experimental research paradigm to study different kinds of questions. And as descriptive studies become more sophisticated, along the lines suggested by Dickinson and Blunt in their chapter, they should yield substantial information about significant relationships among those elements important to adult educators. This development, too, should stimulate greater use of the experimental method, as we attempt to clarify those relationships.

    The research design described in this chapter is that labeled the true experimental design by Campbell and Stanley (1963), to distinguish it from a variety of other designs that will be briefly identified later in the chapter. Although this method is perceived in certain circles as the highest form of scientific inquiry, I am not prepared to accept a hierarchical ordering of research methods, since I believe a variety of approaches is desirable for expanding knowledge. Hence, I regard the experimental research design discussed here as but one available means of testing claims against evidence for the purpose of progressively approximating reality or truth.

Basic Logic and Mill's Canons

Experimental research is enhanced by an awareness of the relationships among logic, Mill's five rules of experimental research, and hypothesis testing. An understanding of logic is necessary in designing a theoretically sound experimental research design. The researcher analyzes and synthesizes theory until he explicates a proposition. That proposition may be defined as a truth statement or a logical consequence. The primary consideration in judging such a proposition is whether or not it conforms to the canons of logic for determining what is true and what is false (Dubin, 1969). Two kinds of propositions have been discussed in the literature—categorical and hypothetical (Dubin, 1969).

The most common form of propositional logic is concerned with establishing the class, or set, of which certain elements are members. The classical categorical syllogism illustrates this kind of analysis, and its use is frequently referred to as the deductive method. When one reasons deductively, one holds that what is true of all instances of a class must also be true of any single instance that comes within its limits. Therefore, one tries to demonstrate that a particular instance under consideration logically falls within the instances of an entire class. To accomplish the deductive objective, one uses the device known as the syllogism.

A syllogism provides a logical means of determining the validity of a particular conclusion or fact. It is an argument of three propositions. The first two statements are premises and furnish the grounds for the conclusion, the third or final proposition. Four kinds of syllogisms have been identified: alternative, categorical, disjunctive, and hypothetical. Here is an example of each kind:

1. Alternative
   Either I will work all day, or I will not finish my work.
   I will not work all day.
   Therefore, I will not finish my work.
2. Categorical
   All humans are mammals (major premise).
   She is a human (minor premise).
   Therefore, she must be a mammal (conclusion).
3. Disjunctive
   It is not the case that one is both a good man and a good
   politician.
   He is a good man.
   Therefore, he is not a good politician.
4. Hypothetical
   If one jumps into a pool of water, he will get wet.
   He jumped into a pool of water.
   Therefore, he got wet.

Each kind of syllogism is characterized by and labeled according to the type of proposition in the major premise. The hypothetical syllogism is especially useful in the search for scientific laws by means of stating and testing hypotheses (Van Dalen, 1973). The hypothetical syllogism requires that the investigator have enough knowledge of an event to discard irrelevant bits of information, to select previously unconnected facts critically, and to combine such facts in a way that implies a conclusion. Deductive reasoning provides a structure for the organization of premises into patterns that provide evidence for the validity of a conclusion.

Even though they differ in appearance and context, syllogisms and statistical procedures share the common functions of classification and inference. For example, statistical procedures are useful to the researcher in determining the appropriate set from which a statistic is derived. Tests of significance are concerned with locating the universe of which a specific statistic is a member. Thus, the means of two samples can be compared statistically to determine the probability that they are from different populations or sets. If the difference between the means exceeds specified limits, then the difference is said to be significant statistically and the two samples are considered to be from different sets.

A theoretical-hypothetical proposition is specifically concerned with a theory in operation, usually with the values of units or concepts in that theory. Such a propositional statement is a prediction, because it tells what must be true about the theory in operation if other elements of the theory are known. Usually the proposition states the values of two critical theoretical units or concepts in the classic "if—then" format. For example: "If an individual has reached a high level of education, then he will participate in a learning activity." This proposition states that a positive value of education is associated with a positive value of learning. Propositions derived from theory provide the basis for hypothetical statements. And every proposition is potentially capable of generating a large number of hypotheses. More is said about hypotheses after a brief look at Mill's canons of experimental research.

The conduct of experimental research is clarified by an understanding of the five methods of John Stuart Mill (Hillway, 1974), whose analysis of experimental research generated four major principles, to which a fifth is added by combining the first two. They are useful guides in the development of a research design, but they should not be dogmatically accepted as rigid rules that must be applied in all cases. These five are (1) the method of agreement, (2) the method of difference, (3) the joint method, (4) the method of residues, and (5) the method of concomitant variations. According to the principle of agreement, if the phenomena leading up to a given event always have only one factor in common, that factor is probably the cause of the specified event. Or when the idea is expressed in the negative, it may be observed that in the absence of a specific factor (X), no combination of phenomena (A + B + C) can be the cause of the identified event (E). The method of difference applies if two or more sets of circumstances are identical except for one factor, and if a specific result occurs only when that factor is present; in this case the factor in question may be the cause of the result. Stated negatively, no factor can be the cause of a phenomenon if the phenomenon occurs in the absence of that factor. The joint method, which incorporates both of the first two methods, perhaps generates more reliable results than either of its components used independently. According to this third method, if the conditions of agreement and the conditions of difference are met, the cause of a given event should be fairly evident (Hillway, 1974). The third principle then requires that one factor common to all instances in which the given phenomenon occurs is present and that the phenomenon never occurs when that particular factor is absent.

Examples of the application of these principles in adult education research are readily available. For instance, Buckholdt and Ferriton (1974) report an investigation that illustrates the idea of the method of agreement. Their study was intended to determine whether the use of a token reinforcement procedure would change two specific behaviors of adult students. And their data suggest that this procedure did effectively explain the observed behavior change. The second method is illustrated by the work of Cole and Glass (1977), who set up an experiment to explain the difference between two groups in terms of a specific variable. They developed an experimental group and a control group to determine how students' participation in program planning affected their achievement, retention, and attitude. The difference between the two groups was subsequently explained by the student-participation variable.

Boshier's study (1975) of the effect of a behavior modification program in a graduate program was designed in such a way as to illustrate the joint method of agreement and disagreement. This canon requires at least two groups with only one circumstance in common and at least two instances in which this circumstance does not occur in order that the two groups will have nothing in common except the absence of that circumstance. Boshier met this requirement by manipulating his sample so that two subgroups each experienced the "treatment" and each served as a control at some point during the study. As a result, Boshier could explain his findings in the presence or absence of the treatment condition. The following diagram illustrates the joint method of agreement as used in Boshier's study. The symbol (+) indicates the presence of the desired behavior; (−) indicates the absence of the desired behavior.

	Conditions	
	Experimental	Control
Group 1	(+)	(−)
Group 2	(+)	(−)

In both instances where the treatment was present, the desired behavior occurred; in both instances where the treatment was absent, the desired behavior failed to occur.

The fourth method, the method of residues, is based on the recognition that some problems cannot be solved by the application of the first three principles. The method of residues may be expressed as follows: "Remove from any phenomena such action as is known by previous analysis to be the effect of certain antecedents, and the residue of the phenomena is the effect of the remaining antecedents" (Cohen and Nagel, 1934, p. 264). The discovery of the planet Neptune is cited as an example of the application of this method. The movements of Uranus had been studied with the help of Newton's theories. Accordingly, the orbit of Uranus was projected on the assumption that the sun and the planets within Uranus's orbit were the only bodies determining its motion. But calculations revealed that Uranus's observed position was different from the theoretical position. It was therefore assumed that the differences could be accounted for only by the gravitational action of another planet. The perturbations in the motion of Uranus were then used to calculate the position of the hypothetical planet. Neptune was subsequently discovered in the vicinity of the place calculated for it (Cohen and Nagel, 1934).

According to the method of concomitant variations, when two phenomena consistently vary together, either the change in the first is caused by the variation in the second or both are changed by some common factor. To illustrate the fifth method, Mill cited the relationship between the moon and earth's tides. The factors, in this case, the moon and tides, are beyond man's ability to manipulate, and thus the methods of agreement, method of difference, and the joint method cannot be used to examine the relationship. However, the method of concomitant variation provides a framework wherein the variations in tides may be compared with the variations in the moon's position relative to the earth. Such observation suggests three possible conclusions: (1) the tides affect the motion of the moon, or (2) the changes in the moon's relationship to the earth affect the tides, or (3) the variations in the moon's position and the changes in the tides are caused by some element affecting both.

Mill's fourth and fifth principles have become preferred bases of analysis in many of the social sciences and in education. Modern developments in statistical analysis, such as factor analysis and multiple correlations, with corollary developments in computer science and technology have increased the utility of the latter principles. Nevertheless, four limitations restrict the use of Mill's principles in modern research. First, they are designed for qualitative dichotomous variables, those which are either usually present or usually absent. Second, they are based on the assumption that no interaction occurs among the variables. Third, they are not efficient, because study is limited to one causal variable at a time. And finally, they fail to take account of random variations in measurement. The simple logic of the principles is both an advantage and disadvantage. The simplicity is attractive, but it sometimes fails to cover adequately complex interactions that exist in reality. For example, causal relations are seldom clear. Furthermore, the qualitative form of the methods may not allow them to be applied effectively to quantitatively determined variables. Modern statistical techniques seem to be related only to the use of Mill's fifth principle, that of concomitant variations, which is seen by some as the logical precursor of modern correlation procedures.

Despite these limitations, however, Mill's canons are instructive in developing an attitude toward the eliminative nature of the experimental research design. The eliminative or disconfirming characteristic of experimental research seems to be closely related to the use of hypothetical statements that lend themselves to testing within the logical framework explicated earlier. Consequently, the logical principle of the excluded middle is that any proposition must be either true or false (Phillips, 1971), and the convention of testing a null hypothesis in order to prove it true or untrue serves the elimination needs of experimental research very well.

Hypotheses

Hypotheses are useful devices to all kinds of individuals seeking solutions to problems. The mechanic, housewife, and carpenter may frequently employ informally stated hypotheses to help organize their thinking in order to solve a problem. When used in experimental research, hypotheses are often formally stated; that is, they are expressed as statements or questions in order to explain, describe, or predict conditions or events that have not been confirmed by facts. The organizational properties of hypotheses require the researcher to restrict the scope of the question under investigation. Through the use of hypotheses the researcher brings together isolated data into some unifying framework. Finally, hypotheses provide the researcher with some direction in identifying relevant information.

Hypotheses may be derived from theory—deductive—or they may be ad hoc, inductive hypotheses. Different scholars prefer one over the other. Many of the hypotheses appearing in adult education research are ad hoc. Such hypotheses are frequently associated with the situation in which an investigator discovers a measuring device, proceeds to use it, and then asks, after identifying some statistical relationship between the values measured, What theory can I relate these findings to? A sustained inductive pursuit of knowledge based on empirical conclusions may be fruitful if it is carried out with reasonable logic. The University of Chicago School of Sociology was characterized by this kind of research between the two world wars (Dubin, 1969).

Hypotheses have been described as bold, descriptive, explanatory, and substantive; a fifth category contains research hypotheses. So-called "bold" hypotheses are those that go beyond available facts in an effort to answer a question. Descriptive hypotheses are intended to answer such questions as what, when, who, and where. In contrast, explanatory hypotheses seek to provide answers to how and why concerns. A substantive hypothesis is a conjectural statement that may be derived from the theory being tested. The substantive hypothesis is not testable until each of its terms is defined operationally. Statistical research hypotheses are commonly tested against a null hypothesis, which states that there is no relation between the variables of a problem. The null hypothesis is a state-ment of chance expectation. It is never completely disproved and its retention or nonrejection is always tentative.

Invalid hypotheses may also prove to be useful in the process of discovering the correct solution to a given problem. Indeed, most problems of consequence have not been resolved by the formulation and testing of a single hypothesis. Theory building usually proceeds slowly through a process of eliminating a series of hypotheses.

To be useful, a hypothesis must have certain characteristics. First, it must be testable. Valid hypotheses are those that have been tested and confirmed by evidence. The difficulty of confirming a hypothesis depends to a large degree on the precision and clarity of the statement. Second, an hypothesis is expected to account for all the facts it purports to cover. Third, it should be able to explain what is claimed for it. And finally, a hypothesis should be internally consistent (Bledsoe, 1972).

The null hypothesis is formulated and tested according to the following procedure (Bledsoe, 1972, p. 56):

1. Report the null hypothesis.
2. Select a statistical technique based on the test that most closely approximates the conditions of the research and whose measurement requirements are met by the research.
3. Select the significance level for rejecting the null hypothesis.
4. Specify the sample size.
5. Find or assume the sampling distribution of the statistical test.
6. On the basis of the chosen statistical technique, the risk of Type I error, the sample size, the sampling distribution, and the alternative hypothesis, define the region of rejection.
7. Determine the value from the statistical test. If the value is in the region of rejection, the null hypothesis should be rejected.
8. Rejection of the null hypothesis results in the acceptance of the alternative hypothesis.

Researchers are constantly alert to two kinds of erroneous conclusions that may result from their work: accepting a null hypothesis that should be rejected, and rejecting a null hypothesis that should be accepted. Because of the implications of such errors, experimental designs are constructed to reduce threats to internal and external validity as much as possible. Concern about internal validity is based on the need to be able to observe that any change in the subject can be explained by the treatment. In contrast, concern about external validity arises from the need to be able to report the populations, settings, treatment, and variables to which the findings can be generalized.

Different kinds of extraneous variables that threaten internal validity have been identified by Campbell and Stanley (1963). Those variables are due to a number of factors:

1. History—the unanticipated and uncontrolled events that occur between the first and subsequent measurement, in addition to those events due to the independent variables.
2. Maturation—biological processes operating as a function of the passage of time.
3. Testing—how the first test affects people's scores on subsequent tests.
4. Instrumentation—changes in the calibration of a measuring device or scale and changes in observers that may influence changes in scores.
5. Statistical regression—the possible effects of the selection process.
6. Selection bias—the impact of sampling procedures.
7. Experimental mortality—the differential loss of respondents from comparison groups.
8. Selection-maturation-interaction—a problem in certain multiple-group designs.
9. Instability—the instability or unreliability of measures.

External validity or representativeness may be threatened by (1) the reactive or interaction effect of testing; (2) the interaction effects of biases in sample selection and the experimental variable; (3) the reactive effects of experimental arrangements; (4) multiple treatment interference; (5) the irrelevant responsiveness of measures; and (6) the irrelevant replicability of treatments.

Kinds of Experimental Designs

Campbell and Stanley (1963) cogently describe the variations available in designing an experimental research project. Tuckman (1972) and Kerlinger (1967) also provide insights on this subject. Reference to those publications should be a normal prelude to planning an experimental research project. Because of the impact of Campbell and Stanley's classification of experimental research designs in educational research, their main ideas are summarized below. They describe sixteen designs divided into four classes: preexperimental (designs 1–3), true experimental (4–6), quasi-experimental (7–10), and correlational and ex post facto designs (11–16).

The three preexperimental designs have severe limitations. The one-shot case study is really a descriptive analysis of a group following some treatment. There is no control group or pretest. The one-group pretest-posttest design also fails to provide a control group. Furthermore, the experimenter has no control over the effects that are due to history, maturation, testing, and instrumentation; and statistical regression may contribute to another explanation of the findings. In the static-group comparison design, an "untreated" group is compared with an experimental group. The results are confounded because of the inability of the researcher to determine that the two groups are equivalent except for the treatment.

The three true experimental designs meet all the first eight threats to internal validity identified by Campbell and Stanley. In contrast, the quasi-experimental designs are characterized by partial control by the researcher. He may have full control over the "when" and "who" measurement elements, but lacks full control over the scheduling of the treatment, including the timing of the treatment as opposed to the timing of the measurement and the random assignment of subjects.

Experimental research is distinguished from other kinds of research by the use of designs that are primarily intended to eliminate rival hypotheses or explanations of cause and effect (invariant relations). In addition, the experimental design is characterized by control groups, randomized samples of subjects (elements), and manipulation (treatment) of independent variables in order to control pertinent factors as much as possible. Furthermore, the independent and dependent variables are frequently operationally defined so they can be described according to a given set of criteria.

A strong experimental design must be carefully conceived and rigorously monitored and controlled because each of its characteristics (control group, randomization, manipulation, and operational definition) affects the validity of the findings. Weaknesses often develop in one of the following ways: the experimenters fail in their efforts to control the environment of the control group adequately; they fail to randomize the experimental group; the manipulated variable is unsatisfactorily handled; or the key variables are not sufficiently operationalized for accurate quantification. Boyd's chapter in this volume points out related issues.

The characteristics of the experimental method (control, randomization, manipulation, and operational definition) are related to two crucial elements of the experiment: (1) the experiment must focus on some specific change that takes place, whether introduced by the investigator or by the environment; and (2) the experimenter must be able to achieve a high degree of control over the experimental condition or to understand the situation well enough to make allowances for relevant factors (Phillips, 1971).

There are basic differences between the class of true experimental designs and the research methods discussed in earlier chapters. For example, the survey method seeks to generate information on the status of a phenomenon, whereas the experimental method is generally concerned with determining the existence of a phenomenon, the cause of the phenomenon, under what kinds of conditions the phenomenon under study may exist, and how a phenomenon may vary systematically in quantity or quality with another phenomenon. Using the grounded-theory method one may attempt to determine similar things, but one would use the inductive approach rather than the deductive approach of the experimental method, and one would be generating hypotheses instead of testing them. The historical method also differs from the experimental method, principally with respect to the researcher's control over the subjects. For example, the experimental researcher usually manipulates some variable in the environment so that the first condition is different from the second condition in a planned and controlled way. The researcher's ability to control selected variables and to account for differences between two groups based on that control is central to the experimental design. But the historian cannot control the subjects or the environment, which have only historical visibility and cannot be manipulated.

Thus, the experimental method cannot be easily confused with other research methods unless one uses the ex post facto or quasi-experimental designs described by Campbell and Stanley (1963). The user of these designs lacks control and usually seeks to explain changes that occur without the investigator's manipulation.

Handling the Critical Elements: Examples

A few examples of how the critical elements—control, randomization, manipulation, operational definition, and the testing of hypotheses—have been handled in adult education studies should prove to be instructive. Because I assume that articles appearing in *Adult Education* are fairly representative of research in the field, I have chosen such articles for illustrative purposes. But since these articles are frequently summarized reports of larger projects and since it is difficult to determine whether the weaknesses noted are products of the report procedure or part of the design, I have not identified the articles and their authors.

The experimenter has available several procedures for controlling the assignment of subjects to appropriate groups. These procedures include administrative selection procedures and statistical techniques. The physical control represented by the administrative selection procedures appears to be generally preferred. But in situations where such control is not possible, the experimenter must use a statistical treatment, such as a partial correlation technique, to hold one variable constant.

One study reported in *Adult Education* achieved control through an administrative procedure. In this study, designed to measure differences in students' achievement produced by two instructional methods, among other things, the control was provided by limiting all enrollment to the experimental and control courses. Thus, students registered in 1966–67 in an experimental class (unknowingly) and in 1967–68 in a control class. Courses at two levels were used; all lower-level courses were experimental one year and control the second year. The opposite sequence was followed in the higher-level courses. There were 322 students in the experimental group and 308 in the control group. The outcomes were analyzed according to sex, credit-hours attempted, semester gradepoint average, cumulative gradepoint average, and pretest scores.

Up to this point, the approach appears to be proper. But another element that needs to be controlled—the similarity of treatment—was apparently not carefully handled. Although each of the nine instructors was to teach both kinds of sections, experimental and control, only five actually did so. And the article does not discuss how the instructors were prepared for the experiment. Their participation, personality, and related classroom interactions thus appear (from the available data) to have been loosely controlled.

This study illustrates how one can provide control in some areas only to lose it in others. Because the instructor variable was apparently poorly controlled, any difference in achievement could be explained as well by the instructor variable as by the experimental treatment. Thus the researcher must examine all elements of any control efforts to ensure the validity of the collected data and the corresponding analyses. Many research problems also require statistical control to make up for administrative deficiencies.

The manipulation of variables is illustrated by a study in which the investigator manipulated several variables at strategic points. First, he obtained one set of data by asking the subjects, on whom he exerted no overt pressure, to respond to a written instrument. Later, he obtained oral responses to identical stimuli when the subjects were under group pressure. He also manipulated the information presented so that each subject responded to two different classes of stimuli and two different kinds of content in each class. Manipulating one variable, such as the instructional method, is usually not overly difficult. But manipulating several variables, such as the kind of information, the group size, the kind of group, and personality characteristics, becomes more difficult. Statistical as well as administrative manipulation is usually required in such complex experiments.

Another study is instructive in the use, or lack of use, of operational definitions. According to the article, the central hypothesis was that the "personality characteristics of participants in management development programs influence the success of the teaching methods used." The investigator then predicted certain results, such as, "The case-discussion method would be more successful than the lecture method for more extroverted people." Although several key words in this sentence are basic to the fundamental objectives and design of the study—"case discussion method," "more successful," "lecture method," "extroverted," and "people"—the author failed to define any of those terms operationally. By studying the procedures, the reader can deduce how extroversion and success were measured and who the people were. However, such failure to define key terms operationally puts a heavy burden on the reader and may affect the interpretation of the results. Even though differences between the lecture technique and case-discussion technique were central concerns, they were not defined. Clearly, operationalism is extremely important in experimental research. Phillips (1971) points out that operationalism is constructive in calling attention to the importance of clarity, precision, and definition.

The stating and testing of hypotheses, the last of the "critical elements" discussed in this section, are not handled consistently in the experimental studies reported in *Adult Education*. Hypotheses have been referred to as "questions put to nature" and as the basic tools of experimental research. And thus most experimental studies are designed to test one or more hypotheses. However, in these articles the number and quality of the hypotheses vary widely. For example, one study contained five hypotheses stated in the null form. The writer also provided the acceptable level of probability. In contrast, another article provided only a substantive hypothesis without indicating the acceptable level of probability.

Only a few adult education dissertations demonstrate the use of the experimental method. For instance, a review of twelve abstracts provided by ERIC revealed few salient characteristics of that method. Five of the dissertations (Bodenhamer, 1964; Dollins,

1967; Etter, 1969; Grotelueschen, 1967; Lupton, 1967) dealt with instruction and three with attitudinal questions (Peters, 1968; Rhyne, 1968). Each of the others took up a different kind of problem: comparing the musical pitch discrimination of adults and children (Maltzman, 1964); examining the relationship between rates of parental participation in education (Majure, 1972); group size and divergent thinking (Shah, 1966); and the information-processing capacity of persons of different ages (Carpenter, 1967). These dissertations are cited not as examples of good or poor design, only as examples of the kinds of dissertations written by adult education students. The reader should review the studies to determine their strengths and weaknesses.

As a consulting editor for *Adult Education*, I have had frequent opportunities to assess research reports from the field. Articles submitted for consideration often suffer from one or more weaknesses with respect to the critical elements of experimental research: (1) External validity is often weakened by the sample-selection procedures. So-called random samples often fail to provide all potential subjects an equal chance of selection. (2) Design difficulties frequently include a lack of control over additional variables (other than treatment), such as education, exposure, maturation, or unique experience. (3) Interpretation error is sometimes in evidence; the experimenter fails to use an appropriate statistical treatment, goes beyond the data, or applies findings to an inappropriate population. One example was provided by a recent manuscript wherein the data called for multivariate analysis, but the experimenter used only univariate analysis. An example of going beyond the data was provided by a manuscript in which the writer arrived at conclusions that did not appear to be supported in the reported findings and that were not related to the design.

Explanations for Limited Use of Experimental Method

Some fields of study and practice, such as psychology, physics, and chemistry, are especially suited to the use of the experimental method. Others—sociology, history, and education, for instance—are not always so amenable to the method. But because of the prestige of such fields as psychology and the natural sciences in academic circles, researchers in other fields are constrained to generate experimental studies as a kind of reputation-maintenance act.

Thus it is no surprise that adult educators, who have at best a marginal status in higher education power circles, have sometimes felt they had to defend their intelligence, scholarship, and analytical rigor by trying to use the experimental method. Knowles (1973) has written pointedly on this situation, and little profit would result from expounding further. However, it is important to observe that adult educators should not feel compelled to select the experimental method just because it is the "in thing." Like any other researchers, they should select the method most appropriate to the problem they are studying. And in fact, they have not felt so compelled, if we are to judge by the assertions of four major sources (DeCrow and Loague, 1970; Dickinson and Rusnell, 1971; Grabowski and Loague, 1970; Long and Agyekum, 1974), who indicate that adult educators have used the experimental research method much less frequently than other methods.

One explanation for this finding may be the humanistic orientation of most adult educators, which may be somewhat in-consistent with the use of the experimental method. Humanists hold that the individual is unique and that efforts to reduce human differences to a quantified continuous scale present logical and philosophical problems. Some adult educators may believe that measures of central tendency fail to measure any individual, and as a result, such measures are not useful. When such limited use is compared with the possible costs of such data, such as the cost of violating the researcher's philosophy regarding the integrity of the individuals tested or treated in an experimental design, the costs may exceed the reward for the researcher. Hence, the experimental method is seldom used by people with such beliefs.

The developmental stage of the field, at which the problems of practitioners are emphasized, may provide a second explanation. It is possible that as the field changes, adult educators will more often find the experimental method appropriate for the sorts of issues they want to investigate. For example, many of the studies concerning participation have been based on descriptive surveys. But to explain how and why participation occurs, investigators must use experimental methods.

Somewhat related to both of the foregoing possibilities is a third explanation: the philosophical orientation and professional concerns of practitioners. During the past half century adult educators have stressed pragmatic and often programmatic matters. As a result, they have been highly interested in describing the dynamic field, whose scope and character appear to require continuing reassessment. Similarly, many of their programmatic concerns appear to be more related to descriptive research methods than to experimental methods, especially when cast against a humanistic orientation. For example, how does one establish or prove the need for continuing education or assess the efficacy of certain administrative procedures by using an experimental design? Until basic questions such as these are more fully understood, adult education may employ experimental research less than other methods.

Another explanation is the kind of research training adult educators receive. Many are not taught how to use experimental designs in adult education research. Most research-design courses the graduate student takes are based on examples and problems more closely related to public schools than to adult education, and sometimes they concern even less meaningful (to adult education students) subjects. As a result, the graduate student in adult education often does not learn about the variety of research models. A related factor is that many graduate advisors are themselves inexperienced in experimental work. This problem can be overcome only as more professors of adult education become competent at experimental research.

Difficulties in formulating theory in adult education may provide the fifth explanation. In the fields in which the experimental design is frequently used, physics and chemistry particularly, theory is highly developed. In contrast, adult education and its generic area, education, have few theoretical foundations. The experimental method as a hypothesis-testing procedure is especially well suited to theoretical fields. Conversely, one could argue that the less theoretical fields are better served by other research designs.

Problems related to the testing of adults provide a sixth potential explanation for the limited use of the experimental method in adult education. Any experimental design that uses human subjects contains a particular set of problems. The problems of control may be described as a continuum on which inanimate subjects present the least difficulties, animals more, children even more, and finally, adults most. Why? For one thing, obtaining permission and cooperation from adults in experimental studies is sometimes difficult. Often, such subjects are a fortuitous voluntary sample, are compensated, and may come from an institutionalized population. All three possibilities have some potential impact on external validity or encourage the selection of another research method. Finally, many adults may find it unrewarding or overly time-consuming to participate in an experimental study. As a result, they may depart from the scene physically or psychologically. Even in those instances when adults are not strongly opposed to the activity, their relative sophistication may motivate them to seek and discover the intent of the experimenter and to behave in such a way as to affect the outcomes. Consequently, the validity of the findings may be low.

A study cited earlier (the one involving the use of nine instructors each year for two years) also illustrates another problem: research that requires an extended time. In this case, the research plan was aborted when four of the nine instructors left before the study was completed.

Factors Favoring Use of the Experimental Method

Whatever the explanations for its limited use at present, the experimental method should prove more attractive to adult educators in the future for four main reasons.

First, the field has, I believe, reached a state of development that requires the testing of hypotheses. Although the dynamic character of adult education will probably necessitate further efforts to describe and define its characteristics and boundaries, we also need to examine deeply specific topics as a means to better understanding and increased knowledge. And such in-depth study will require manipulation of some variables.

The special subjects needing examination include adult learning, instructional strategies and modes, delivery systems, and learner motives. The literature is replete with case analyses and descriptions of teaching techniques, but almost barren of experiments measuring interactions among learning styles, methods and techniques, and learner motives.

The increased use of the experimental method in adult education has important implications for the theoretical development of the field, since that growth may very well depend on how much scientific inquiry contributes to the discovery of useful ideas and to their evaluation. Adult educators are interested in strategies that will help to develop ideas contributing to scientific progress. And because not every idea that is generated is worthwhile, they are also interested in evidence and judgments concerning the value of ideas (Phillips, 1971). Tests (experimental research) within the latter context suggest the direction of further inquiry. Evidence presented in this evaluative context not only may indicate that the ideas are potentially fruitful, but may also suggest what kinds of additional data are urgently needed. Conversely, if evidence indicates that the ideas are incorrect, the experimenter is driven to make discoveries.

The experimental method and theory formulation are closely related. The experimental design is perhaps of greatest value when the investigator has developed a theory and wishes to validate it. If this perception is correct, efforts to develop theory in adult education should be followed by efforts to validate that theory. Thus, the advancement of a validated theoretical base in adult education requires the execution of experimental research.

Economics is a second factor favoring the use of the experimental research methods by graduate students in adult education. If the researcher can readily identify and secure access to a group of adults, the research with these people may be less expensive in time and money than a study using historical or grounded theory methods. However, the costs will vary among the research methods as well as within any method, according to the design and nature of the study.

The relative ease of reporting the findings of an experimental study also favors an increase in such work. As indicated previously, a characteristic of the experimental method is the generation of quantified data that are often used to test hypotheses. In most dissertation studies the decision to reject a hypothesis is easily made following statistical analyses. That decision, in turn, usually leads directly to conclusions that can be supported by the quantified data.

There is a certain degree of security in such data that may be especially appealing to the graduate student. Conclusions in studies based on other methods are not always so clean-cut. For example, the historian's data may always be subject to the question whether the sources are biased or whether the researcher was biased in selecting and interpreting the material. Similar questions of interpretation also apply to other research methods.

A warning may be required here, however. There is a rather close relationship among hypotheses, theory, and explanation. Scientific explanations usually describe the relationship between at least two variables. These explanations are based on the evidence for such relationships (Phillips, 1971). Explanation is thus hindered or assisted by the evidence generated and the theoretical framework guiding the development and implementation of the research design. Therefore, although the presentation of findings may be relatively easy, suitable explanation and interpretation may be more difficult.

A fourth factor favoring the use of the experimental method is the clarity of the design. The experimental design is usually easy to describe. The graduate student can tell in parsimonious terms how he will treat group A as opposed to group B and how the quantified differences between the two groups will be analyzed. The task of writing a dissertation based on the experimental method may therefore be less difficult than writing one based on other designs.

Thus, there are several acceptable explanations for the limited number of adult education dissertations based on the experimental design. And there are also a number of rather good reasons why graduate students in adult education may wish to consider an experimental design.

Need for Experimental Research

Experimental research in adult education does not appear to suffer more from design weaknesses than do other forms of research. So I want to point out once again that adult education will probably be best served by the use of a variety of techniques. The selection of the appropriate method needs to be determined by several factors. For example, if independent variables can be manipulated or controlled, the experimental method might be appropriate. If only highly select volunteer subjects are available, or if manipulation is impossible, the experimental method is probably inappropriate.

The number of experimental studies in adult education has gradually increased in recent years. The increase parallels developments occurring among the practitioners, as well as changes in adult educators' research competence. These kinds of modifications will probably speed up too, thus contributing to further use of the experimental method. And the development of inferential statistics and multivariate techniques of analysis, accompanied by the development of computer technology, including packaged computer programs, may help overcome some of the problems of control and analysis.

Unfolding areas in adult education call for the use of all available research skills and methods. If the field is to develop in substance as well as size, such variety is imperative. Adult educators are called on to be realistic in their assessment of research needs. Careful, rigorous, ethical experimental research is necessary (in combination with other kinds of research) if adult education is to develop. Descriptive research can go only so far before continued application becomes redundant. Unprofitable redundancy may be prevented if there is close interaction among the research methods and mutual respect among the practitioners. Thus, graduate students, practitioners, and professional researchers in adult education are encouraged to carefully examine the experimental method in their attempts to extend knowledge of adult education.

Chapter Seven

Central Issues in Scientific Methodology

Robert D. Boyd

This chapter is not intended to cover all the major issues of scientific methodology but rather to discuss those that I have observed to be most frequently misunderstood. The topics considered here unavoidably overlap subjects discussed elsewhere in the book, because these issues are obviously interrelated. Nevertheless, I hope my particular perspective on them will prove useful to adult education researchers. My positions on these matters may not entirely agree with those taken by other contributors to the book, and thus I urge the reader to carefully examine the complementary and contrasting positions on logical grounds compatible with scientific investigation.

These issues are taken up in a number of scholarly and informative books, some of which are cited in the References. In particular I recommend two encyclopedic sources for the adult educator who is interested in pursuing a personal reading program in the nature, practice and problems of research: Buros (1972) and Lake, Miles, and Earle (1973). In this chapter, however, certain of the central problems dealt with extensively in other works are restated in a concise and integrative manner. In addition, I relate these issues to the actual doing of research in adult education. For this reason, I present illustrations—often drawn from the broader fields of education and psychology—throughout the chapter, in an attempt to whet the reader's interest in further study.

The two major interrelated problems in adult education research examined in this chapter are theoretical frameworks and methodological difficulties.

Theoretical Frameworks

In discussing theoretical frameworks, writers usually give scant attention to the psychological and social motives that prompt research. And although such motives are legitimate subjects of inquiry in themselves, the focus of this chapter is not on why individuals engage in empirical studies but on how and what methods are used. These two aspects of research must be clearly differentiated.

Conjecture. The formal phase of scientific research begins with a conjecture, a universal statement that sets forth a speculative proposition. It is a universal statement, in contrast to a singular statement, in that it does not deal with a specific event, situation, or relationship. An example of a conjecture is this: Severe inflation in a democratic state during an election year brings the opposition party into power. Conjectures are not whims or flights of fancy; any conjecture proposed as a serious scientific explanation is grounded in some theoretical framework, which is constructed of logical assumptions and propositions and the careful specification of central terms. Frequently, but not necessarily, the framework is supported by empirically accepted data. As an illustration, consider the following hypothetical case.

An adult educator who has made use of small groups has begun to wonder whether he is making the best use of the technique. (Here is the motive, but it has no part in the formal considerations involved in doing scientific research.) Thinking about his problem, he identifies his major concern: how to compose the best instructional groups. Since he has no sound hunches (no conjectures) to guide him, he decides to go to the literature. His reading reveals many insights, not the least of which is that existing research does not provide a clear answer. Now challenged to seek answers by conducting his own research, he phrases his concern as a question: What membership composition will produce the greatest amount of learning, satisfaction, and self-esteem? The question defines the general area of the problem, but it does not provide a workable guide for doing research. What is needed is a conjecture, a statement about what the educator believes to be the best membership composition. From a reading of the literature he proposes that the best groups are those whose members complement each other.

Once the initial conjecture has been made, one might assume that the researcher is ready to begin developing his research design. But he had better be careful, for it is at this point that he may unwittingly fall into a fundamental methodological blunder: letting the theoretical framework dictate the method. This warning may seem contradictory in light of my argument that a theoretical framework is necessary. The quesion naturally arises, What difference does it make if the theoretical framework does dictate the method?

The theory of operant conditioning can be used to illustrate the answer. In this case the conjecture is that if a researcher provides positive reinforcement to a given sequence of behavior, he can shape a behavior pattern. To test the proposition, he sets up a situation in which he can control reinforcement and behavior. For instance, every time an adult student states his position on a value-laden assertion made by the researcher acting as instructor, the researcher praises the adult's behavior. All other responses are ignored. The researcher assumes that this method tests the theory of operant conditioning, but it does not test the theory or, more specifically, the conjecture set forth above. Why not? Because the method is synonymous with the theory: both the theory and the method propose that if you do x, you get y, but there is nothing in the method that eliminates the possibility that other factors as well as x can produce y. Thus if the proposition is that y can only be brought about by doing x, the researcher should set up an experiment in which x is absent and test for the presence of y. More specifically, the conjecture should be stated as follows: Desired behavior patterns cannot be shaped in the absence of positive reinforcers. The method must test the conjecture and be in harmony with the theoretical framework on which the conjecture is based but never be synonymous with the conjecture.

Another way to put this problem is to say that the researcher should not try to verify the conjecture but to falsify it. The certainty of proof is illusory. All one can do is either show the conjecture to be false or fail to show that it is false. The method of *falsifiability* requires that the conjecture be stated in such a manner that it denies the possibility of a given outcome. This notion of falsifiability may be entirely new to the reader, and yet its central place in doing science cannot be ignored. Exploring the idea in depth would go far beyond the scope of this chapter, which can only sketch its outlines. Those who wish to pursue the principle in greater detail, can find a brilliant presentation in Popper's book *The Logic of Scientific Discovery* (1959).

If proof is necessary to verify a conjecture, and if proof is defined as sufficient evidence to establish truth, and if truth, in turn, is an absolute, then it logically follows that there is no proof in scientific enterprises, because there is no current means by which to assign an absolute quality to any human experience. But a researcher can be certain at a given time that there is evidence to show a statement to be false. This point may be stated in another way: If universal statements or conjectures are tested by means of singular statements (statements about events) that have been included in the proof of a given conjecture, one can never assert that the conjecture has been proven. One may, however, be assured that the researcher has not yet falsified the conjecture. Although this is a basic proposition, it is not as central to the present discussion as one that refers directly to method: A method must be established to test that which is denied by the theory rather than to look for that which the theory predicts. And thus preceding such a method must be a testable conjecture, a conjecture that puts a theory in jeopardy. The conjecture takes the form of a universal statement which denies the possibility of some condition or event.

This can be exemplified by the hypothetical adult education study described above, in which the researcher proposed that the most effective instructional groups would be those whose members complement each other. The definition or characteristics of complementarity must be based on some theoretical framework. Of course, the measure of most effective would have to be defined operationally as well, but for the purposes of the example only the operational definition of complementarity will be discussed. In this case the rearcher decides to use the epigenetic theory of psychosocial development set forth by Erikson (1950) as the source of his definition. He then focuses on what he considers to be his major conjecture, asserting that those groups whose members are working on similar identity crises will be the most complementary and therefore highest-achieving, or "best," groups. With this conjecture, he also denies that a group constituted of members working on dissimilar identity crises will compose the highest-achieving group. In terms of my foregoing argument, the researcher should be equally interested in both types of group. It would be incorrect to think of the group whose members have dissimilar identity crises as the control group. Actually, both such groups are the experimental groups.

The use of a null hypothesis is in agreement with the idea of falsifiability. The problem with a null hypothesis is simply that it does not provide the severest test of the theory. The null hypothesis states that there will be no difference between E, the experimental population given treatment T, and E_1, the control population which does not receive treatment T. If no significant difference (defined in some acceptable manner) is found (either in favor of or against treatment T), that part of the theory which concerns treatment T is dismissed with respect to the particular variables examined in the experiment. There is no question that this is a form of falsifying a hypothesis. The more severe test, however, would be to deny that population E_1 could achieve equality with population E. This is to say, the researcher would deny that population E_1 could produce the results which treatment T is designed to develop.

In this connection, I should clarify the difference between a conjecture and a hypothesis. I have spoken of the former as a universal statement, but a hypothesis is also a universal statement.

The difference is not in any quality of universality but in the quality of refinement. A conjecture is a broad statement setting forth a theoretical proposition. A hypothesis sets forth the specific criteria with which one determines whether the statement has been falsified or corroborated. The terms *conjecture* and *hypothesis* are used with these meanings throughout the chapter.

Relation of Concepts and Methods. Theoretical concepts are not insular; their meanings arise from and exist in particular theoretical frameworks. And yet the research literature is replete with examples of researchers who are investigating concept *x* moving back and forth among findings from studies based on theories A, B, and C, without attempting to resolve the ontological and epistemological conflicts that clearly exist among the theories. The problem is evident not only in the work of novices but in the work of recognized scholars such as Ausubel (1968). In discussing the concept of anxiety, Ausubel attempts to relate findings from research on such diverse theories or fields as neobehaviorism, cognitive psychology, field psychology, and ego psychology. He makes no attempt either to reconcile the conflicts among the salient assumptions of the various theories or to examine the different specifications of anxiety.

To avoid such a basic error, one must examine two central points. First, one must realize, and make decisions on this basis, that concepts are, as I have said, theoretical constructs and as such are inescapably embedded in a theoretical framework. A researcher must not be deceived by believing that because the concepts are presented using identical words, their meanings are also identical. Concepts do not transcend theories. And second, the researcher must therefore take great care in selecting instruments based on theories different from the theory he is employing in structuring his project. He must avoid choosing an instrument that manifests a conflict between the assumptions of the theory on which the instrument is based and the assumptions of the theory used in his study.

These two points can be readily illustrated by means of the case of the hypothetical researcher presented above. In that case, the final conjecture was that groups composed of members working on dissimilar identity crises will reach a lower level of achievement than groups whose members have similar identity crises. Now his problem is to identify the means of collecting data. To do so, he needs to determine the identity crises of those participants who will be included in the study. The researcher may first think of an interview as a means of collecting data. He may believe that by developing an interview schedule designed to get at aspects of each of the eight epigenetic stages, he might get his subjects to provide the necessary information. Aside from the matter of rapport and the need for carefully structured questions in the interview schedule (discussed later), the issue is the compatibility between instrumentation and theory. The interview initially appears to have merit, because adult educators know from past research that adults generally are more receptive to an interview than to a pencil-and-paper instrument. However, the proposed procedure has a basic flaw: the assumption that the participants are able to reveal their identity crises to the interviewer through self-examination. Such an assumption ignores the theory of the unconscious, which is an essential aspect of ego psychology, on which Erikson's epigenetic stages are based. The researcher must employ a data-collection technique that takes into account the unconscious state. To make use of any instrument that fails to account for unconscious motivation immediately jeopardizes the validity of the data. Again, there must be complete harmony between the data-gathering instruments and the theory which serves as the framework for the study. The key point in this example is that whatever method of data collection is employed, it must allow for the theoretical assumptions related to the variables which are being measured or it will be invalid theoretically.

Methodological Difficulties

Reliability and Validity. Any serious discussion of method leads to the issues of reliability and validity, because of the central questions these two ideas raise in scientific research. The need for reliability focuses the researcher's attention on matters of stability and dependability. The word *stability* here refers to obtaining similar data over time. Dependability is used in the sense of trustworthiness;

that is, the observations of judge A are to be counted on as being accurate within some acceptable limits.

Validity is an elusive idea. The issue specified by the term *validity* is whether or not the data in some instances can be presumed to be empirical evidence of the variable being examined. The researcher may argue on the grounds of four kinds of validity: concurrent, construct, content, or predictive validity. 'Concurrent validity has to do with two sets of data, one of which has already received some acceptance as being what it is supposed to be. Construct validity concerns a theoretical relationship between the variable under study and another variable that has a better established empirical base; the validity of the first variable is asserted to rest on the existence of the conjectured relationship. Content validity, sometimes referred to as face validity, is based on establishing an isomorphic relation between, for instance, a test item and the content from which the item was drafted. Predictive validity has to do with the correspondence between the scores on the variable proposed on a predictor and subsequent scores on the variable of predicted performance; that is, between scores on a representative sample taken at one time and a performance sample taken later.

This introduction to reliability and validity is intended only as the barest reorientation. If the review confuses more than it enlightens, the reader may find it helpful to read one of several good references, such as Cronbach (1969), Festinger and Katz (1953), Selltiz and others (1959), and Stanley (1969). The discussion here takes up the specific issues researchers encounter in considering questions of reliability and validity in actual empirical studies.

As indicated, reliability connotes stability and dependability. The need to be concerned about stability does not mean, however, that all data must be stable in the sense that over an extended period a researcher will get the same answers to the same questions. If one holds that human development is manifested in different sets of interests, it would be illogical to expect certain human-development variabilities to be stable, since they are expected to change. The important point is that stability must be viewed within the theoretical framework on which the study is based. If one specifies that the variable x within the theoretical framework is constant, then one would expect that two administrations of a self-report instrument, at time A and time B, would produce very similar data. However, one should not conclude from this discussion that a researcher can dismiss the issue of stability when a developmental theory is employed. The investigator is still responsible for reporting on the stability of the data. His or her task is to specify the limits of the period in which the same answer should be expected to be given to the same question. The researcher's specification is based on the theoretical framework of the study. There are certain established ways to examine the stability of the data; the means employed depend on how the data are related to the conjecture being tested. My objective here is simply to point out the methodological obligation of the researcher.

If the conjecture posits little room for error, the reliability test the researcher uses should permit only a small margin of difference between the sets of data. For example, in the study of instructional groups, one might conjecture that the ideas of low-status members will never lead the group toward new discussion topics. The judges employed to identify the initiation of new topics within instructional groups should reach total agreement if the data are not to be contaminated by differences in the coders' judgments. Just as the definition of stability completely reflects pertinent aspects of the study's theoretical framework, so the selection of reliability tests must be made on the basis of meeting the data demands of the conjecture. There is a congruent relationship among the concept of stability, the reliability test, and the theoretical framework. And the researcher is obligated to develop that relationship in his research project. Particular procedures for examining reliability can be found in such valuable sources as Cronbach (1969) and Guetzkow (1950).

The issue of the dependability of the data brings the researcher directly to the problem of possible false answers by a respondent. Dependability, as I pointed out earlier, is an aspect of reliability. Can one depend on the data's being accurate? If an individual from whom a researcher is collecting data chooses not to provide accurate information, then of course the data will not be accurate. That is a serious problem. The researcher, however, should not immediately conclude that an individual has supplied a false answer simply because the researcher finds conflicting pieces of data.

For example, if at a given time an individual reports that he had difficulty with mathematics, the researcher may expect that adult to say that he also had difficulty with arithmetic. If the adult fails to do so at a later time, the researcher may conclude that the adult was not consistent in the answers he gave and obviously was providing a false answer. The researcher's conclusion may be correct. However, before accepting it, the researcher needs to consider the following questions: (1) Does the participant view x (arithmetic) as a subset of y (mathematics)? (2) Are the questions phrased identically, and does the subject perceive them as being identically phrased? And (3), is there a possibility that the participant's original answer was insufficiently differentiated? (As he thought about it, he began to see that the difficulty he had experienced was with algebra, and he actually even enjoyed geometry and arithmetic.) The point is that the investigator should not immediately perceive one of two conflicting answers to be purposely false. The problem may be in the structure of an interview question or a questionnaire item.

This example illustrates the reason for pretesting all data-gathering devices. In scientific research, the question of the credibility of data-gathering instruments and procedures is crucial. Another essential aspect of credibility is the question "Are the data that the researcher proposes to collect directly related to the conjecture?" This, of course, brings us back once again to the issue of validity. Validity is a more fundamental problem than reliability, because the reliability of the data would not matter if the data could not be used in a direct test of the conjecture.

Earlier I identified four kinds of validity: concurrent, construct, content, and predictive. Each is influenced by some common factors, and although I discuss these factors in relation to content validity, I want to remind the reader that they are also important in connection with other kinds of validity.

As the researcher concerns himself with instrument validity, he must examine how well a sample represents some general class. Thus, an achievement-test item that has been drawn from part of the subject matter of a course is assumed to represent the cluster of information from which the item was drawn. Understanding the appropriate use of content validity in the development of instrumentation is essential. For example, let us return to the earlier conjecture that instructional groups whose members are working on dissimilar identity crises will reach a lower level of achievement than groups whose members have similar identity crises. Using Erikson's theory, the researcher derives sets of specifications for eight epigenetic identity crises and, with much work, develops statement items that express those unique specifications. Each of these steps must be subjected to tests of validity. In the first step the researcher writes the specifications and then must determine whether these are correct in terms of the theory from which he has drawn them. Accordingly, he gives the specifications to two or more judges, who decide on their correctness. If the judges are in total agreement, the researcher is ready to move on to the second step— testing the statement items developed from these specifications. This time the researcher asks the judges to determine whether each item is (1) an aspect of the eight crises, (2) classified in the category for which it was designed, and (3) exclusive—that is, it cannot be classified in more than one category.

Clearly, the production of an instrument, as far as content validity is concerned, is generally a very difficult undertaking. And thus it is naive to believe that the first attempt will produce success. In the case study discussed above, the investigator used judges to determine content validity. This is a common practice, and one that raises two issues that should be examined before I extend the discussion of validity. One issue has to do with the word *objectivity* and the other with *intersubjective*. The two are interwoven, but I shall discuss each separately at first in order to highlight specific points.

Objectivity and Intersubjectivity. The pursuit of objectivity is based on the same order of mistaken conception as the pursuit of proof. The idea of objectivity, as if it were above or outside or separate somehow from people, is a fantasy which has too long intruded into the efforts of persons attempting to do scientific research. All data, in the final analysis, rest on interpretations, and interpretations are the product of individuals. This may strike the reader as an extreme position. Yet there appears to be no way of escaping the conclusion that the interpretation of data depends on the agreement that can be achieved among knowledgeable persons. What was accepted as objective truth at the time of Newtonian physics is, of course, rejected today. The objectivity was based on Newton's ability to convince a group of knowledgeable persons that his interpretations accounted for more acceptable observations than did the existing theory. Two educational psychologists can perceive what may be assumed to be a mutually observed event. And yet their interpretations may differ fundamentally. A psychologist who upholds operant conditioning will not see the same event as a cognitive psychologist. This is so, at least in the manner in which each describes the event.

Reaching the truth or being objective is also a problem faced by legal systems. In British and American law, the solution adopted is in essence identical to that which has been accepted by the world of science: the mechanism of the jury. In both cases the criteria are similar. The jury must be thoroughly informed or knowledgeable, must possess the attitude of open-mindedness, and must apply the test of falsifiability to all conjectures and proofs set before it.

The reader may not, as yet, see the need of questioning the status of objectivity. He may believe that objectivity is determined through carefully structured definitions or through mechanistic devices. But anyone who believes that one can achieve objectivity through such means is either failing to see the situation for what it is or refusing to accept it. The pursuit of definitions can be readily shown to be rooted in operationalism. The doctrine of operationalism has merit if it is not pushed to its logical extension. Definitions must be established at some level by a set of conventions agreed upon by a jury of knowledgeable persons; otherwise, the problem becomes one of definitions ad infinitum. In somewhat poetic terms, the problem is that there is no means known by which one may escape from the boundaries of his being. This problem and others of a philosophical nature are treated extensively in the following references, which deal with scientific explanation: Berger and others (1962), Dewey and Bentley (1949), Kaufmann (1968), Lakatos and Musgrove (1970), Mandler and Kessen (1959), Popper (1959), Sherwood (1969), and Stogdill (1970). Likewise, the use of mechanical instrumentation does not provide a way out of the problem. Few, if any, researchers in the field of adult education employ such gadgetry as galvanoscopes, electroencephaloscopes, and impulse recorders. But if an investigator were to do so in the belief that this would bring an objectivity that eliminates the human dimension, he need only be reminded that the reading of the records made by these machines is done by humans. So at this point the researcher again faces the problem of definitions. In addition, this person should not overlook the intersubjective agreements that were required in determining the utility of constructing mechanical and nonmechanical data-collection instruments.

Earlier I argued that although there is no way yet known to identify what is true, there are means by which to recognize what is false. Reality is similar to truth in this respect. As one cannot be certain of knowing truth, one cannot be sure of knowing reality. The establishment of what may be termed reality depends on public agreement on a set of criteria and on the sharing of what may be provisionally called mutual observations (Dewey and Bentley, 1949). Since that idea is fundamental to understanding my position on reality and to the acceptance of intersubjective reality, it should be carefully reexamined. In the briefest terms, no one person has a special talent for identifying and knowing reality. What sense of reality there is comes into being by intersubjective (people-to-people) agreement on a set of criteria. For example, in scientific research one criterion is the establishing of conjectures that can be falsified. Observations corroborate or falsify one's sense of reality. But reality, as far as knowing it is concerned, is arrived at intersubjectively. Therefore, the reader-researcher should focus on developing good intersubjective agreements.

Categorization. The methodological issue for scientific research becomes the level of intersubjective agreement that is appropriate for the conjectures that are being tested. However, regardless of the level which is proposed as acceptable, certain criteria must be met in structuring one's data-gathering procedures. Categorization is basic to any form of intersubjective agreement that may be reached. In structuring categories the researcher must face and handle the demands of two criteria—the exclusiveness and inclusiveness of data.

The criterion of exclusiveness is met when one can demonstrate that the characteristics defining any single category do not overlap the characteristics of any other category within a given category system. In category A the characteristics $A_1A_2...A_n$ are not included as characteristics of category B, which has its own attributes $B_1B_2...B_n$. The criterion of inclusiveness demands that the category system applied to a specified type of data account for all the data within that category system. For instance, to specify the steps in problem solving, one must be able to classify all problem-solving behaviors.

In the development of a category system, a researcher must draw upon a theoretical framework to establish the boundaries and to identify the distinguishing characteristics of each class. The defense of these boundaries is based on the specifications derived from the theory. Thus, the next step is the development of the exclusive categories. It consists of submitting the specifications of the categories to a set of judges whose task is to determine whether any of the categories overlap. If they find no overlapping, the categories have met the criterion of exclusiveness.

The criterion of inclusiveness is satisfied in a similar manner. Again, starting with the theoretical framework, the researcher develops a category system which, in effect, he asserts accounts for all behaviors of a given type. There are two points at which the assertion of inclusiveness may be challenged. First, observations by other researchers may suggest categories that are not included in the system. For example, the theory of operant conditioning does not account for repression as a mode of forgetting. Those psychologists who take the position that they can demonstrate repression reject the category system proposed by proponents of the operant-conditioning theory. The second point at which the assertion of inclusiveness may be challenged is in the actual use of the category system. In this phase of testing the category system, the researcher's policy should always be to provide the judges with an empty-cell category. That is, if there are ten categories in the system, the judges should be provided with an eleventh cell for those data they find do not fit into any one of the ten designated categories. The judges are encouraged to try to falsify the category system by identifying data for all eleven cells. If the judges identify data for each of the ten cells and none for the eleventh, then the researcher assumes that the category system has met the criterion of inclusiveness.

The procedures outlined above are the minimum essential steps to be taken if an attitude of scientific inquiry is to be reflected in method. Specifically, a researcher's obligation is to attempt to provide the means by which to falsify his research decisions, for this is the only tenable scientific stance that is at present open to anyone who attempts to provide scientific explanations.

Validity of Data. The discussion so far has treated the issue of content validity in relation to the instruments a researcher may use in a research project. The validity of instruments is one aspect of the issue of validity, but it does not concern the validity of the data in relation to the conjectures being tested. That is, the data that are being collected must provide evidence to test the hypotheses that have been proposed. The instrument that a researcher proposes to use may have a high degree of validity but be inappropriate for testing the study's hypotheses.

The significance of data validity must be stressed in a discussion of method for researchers in adult education. A survey of research studies in education will reveal numerous instances in which the investigator attempted to prove a causal relationship between treatment A and learning B when, in fact, a host of other factors bear heavily on the outcomes. The researcher may try to handle these factors by randomization and establishing experimental and control groups. Even then, most studies fail to identify a significant difference. One simple explanation is that students who want to learn will do so, even against barriers which have been accidentally or purposely established. However, suppose that a significant difference between the experimental and control groups is found. Does such difference therefore provide corroborative evidence for the conjecture that group achievement improves with the treatment? The reader should quickly identify a design limitation. Randomization is a means to overcome the confounding effects of variables that cannot be systematically controlled or whose effects cannot be experimentally determined. The problem faced by many research designers is that randomization cannot be employed because they are only interested in investigating the differences between two specific and small groups.

This discussion should not lead the reader to conclude that I oppose correlational and similar studies in adult education. The purposes and values of correlational studies are not the focus of attention here. I want to note in passing, however, that correlation studies are most helpful in giving both direction and refinement to certain kinds of inquiry at the early stages of their development. The central point that must not be lost sight of is that a correlational study cannot yield explanations of causal relationships. The fundamental issue is the researcher's responsibility to demonstrate clearly the validity of the data in terms of the direct testing of the conjectures.

Content validity has been examined in relation to several basic issues. The other types of validity have received little attention, although the issues that have been examined apply as well in most cases to concurrent, construct, and predictive validity. The many topics covered by these various types of validity will not be pursued in depth in this chapter, but a brief discussion of construct validity will serve to highlight a basic issue that has been viewed from another perspective earlier in this chapter.

Construct Validity. Construct validity is rarely discussed in adult education research reports. This is unfortunate, as it is a powerful and theoretically important type of validity. The question may then be raised, Why is it not discussed more often? Although there has been no systematic effort that would answer the question, one might suggest an answer from a cursory reading of the adult education research literature. Such an examination reveals that many authors of empirical studies give little or no attention to examining, testing, or developing theoretical frameworks. These researchers launch an investigation of a certain type of phenomena without reporting their place in the continuity of testing and developing theories. Even in the published reviews of articles on empirical studies the authors fail to identify the theoretical threads which tie the series of studies to a conceptual framework. The persons who carry out these empirical studies appear to assume that pieces of information produce knowledge and to forget that the empirical data are at best only a proxy for a mental construct which is an element of a theory. But to assume that knowledge is produced in an additive manner is to overlook a very simple but fundamental proposition: ideas, facts, insights, and awareness are put together only when one or more organizing principles exist. The phenomenon of forgetting the existence of unhappy events was well known before Freud, but it was Freud who suggested the organizing principles of repression. And the works of Bruner, Goodnow, and Austin (1962), Piaget (1960), and Rapaport (1959), among others, also argue the existence of organizing structures.

Although the failure of adult education researchers to seek this type of validity is regrettable, its limited appearance in the literature points to a more serious issue, which I have already referred to. Many research studies in adult education are reported as if they had no ties to a theoretical base. This failure to link an empirical investigation to a theoretical framework may indicate that the investigator is unaware of the relationship between his study and other studies related to the same theoretical base. The absence of such a link constitutes a hiatus in the advancement of cumulative knowledge.

Instrument Development and Testing. The development and testing of instruments is another area that deserves attention in this chapter. It is a vast subject on which many excellent works have been written, and those who wish to do research should take the time to familiarize themselves with the literature. Among these works are Borgatta and Bohrnstedt (1970), Cronbach (1969), Festinger and Katz (1953), Gage (1962), Lindzey (1960), Selltiz and others (1959), Stephenson (1958), Thorndike (1971), and Travers (1964).

A researcher often discovers that the particular type of data-gathering procedure he requires has not been reported in the literature. He then faces a crucial decision: should the project be abandoned because appropriate instruments do not exist, or should he push on and attempt to develop the needed instruments? The decision should receive very careful review. If the researcher contemplates the development of instruments, he should first seek the advice of competent persons. The plural, persons, is used advisedly. The value of jury decisions has been pointed out elsewhere in the chapter. The rigorous development of instruments for data-gathering purposes necessitates tests of reliability and validity. In addition, the researcher must argue the case that the newly developed instruments gather the appropriate data to test the conjectures. These steps demand a great deal of work and should not be taken without full awareness of the effort required.

Data may be collected in several modes. Observations, interviews, historical analysis, self-reports, and projective techniques are the major types available to adult education researchers. Observations, certain types of interviews, and projective techniques make use of judges or coders. When using coders, the researcher must collect information on their training, on their competence, and on intercoder reliability. He must have acceptable assurance that they know what they are doing, that their performance is up to a conventional standard, and that their biases are not so discrepant that each is giving a different interpretation to the same set of data. The procedures involved in selecting, training, and assessing the performance of judges and coders are both costly and time consuming.

Another way to gather data is to have the participants report on themselves by means of either direct self-reports or one or more projective techniques. Self-report formats fall into two major classes, namely, questionnaires and S or Q sorts. Among the many questionnaire types are the Likert Scale, dyadic and multiple-choice, sentence-completion, ranking, and matching-sets questionnaires. Each has advantages and disadvantages that are determined by the given aims, situations, participants, and research resources. S and Q sorts can also be structured in a number of ways. Not only may distributions be modified, but various steps may be introduced to determine the types of sorting that may be done. At present the Likert Scale questionnaire has a statistical procedural advantage over the other self-report instruments. Computer programs provide simple and direct methods by which to check the interitem reliability of an instrument. This is a feature that cannot be readily ignored. Other interitem reliability procedures are available, but there is none at present that can be applied to data from an S or Q sort that employs a normal distribution. The difficulty can be handled in a reasonably defensible manner. S- or Q-sort items can be structured in a Likert Scale schedule. Data from the administration of this schedule can then be submitted to the interitem reliability programs to determine the interitem reliability of the item statements. Although the need to clearly specify the variables in any study has been stressed previously, it may be of value to review this point in the context of developing a self-report instrument. Clear specification of each variable is essential to the construction of any self-report instrument. When the items—that is, the individual statements—have been written, they must be submitted to a jury of knowledgeable judges to determine their inclusive and exclusive properties. Undoubtedly, some items will have to be reworked, others discarded, and new items developed. The instrument should not be considered completed until the judges agree about each item.

This discussion of data-gathering devices has only touched on a selected and limited number of issues dealing with instrumentation. In conclusion, I want to stress that although rigorous examination of research instruments is important, it would be sad and unfortunate if such concerns were to frighten off attempts at creative efforts.

Summary

Two major problems are evident in far too many emipircal studies reported in the educational-research literature. The first is that researchers fail to establish an appropriate theoretical background for their studies. Consequently, they fail to integrate their studies in coherent and consistent conceptual frameworks. In adult education the problem is even more severe. Studies are proposed without any reference to a theory. Inevitably, it is there implicitly, and in most cases, the unstated framework is an assortment of conflicting assumptions. The second problem concerns a host of difficulties with methods. If adult educators are to make their scientific research more sophisticated, they will have to address these two problems.

Chapter Eight

Trends in Graduate Research

Stanley M. Grabowski

Are there discernible trends in adult education graduate research? Knowles (1973) has suggested that a field of study such as adult education may go through developmental stages. If he is correct, graduate research may reflect gross trends in the field. And if dissertations reflect trends, such information should be instructive for all adult education researchers. The purpose of this chapter is therefore to analyze graduate research in adult education since 1935, with a particular emphasis on the late sixties and early seventies. Attention is focused on the quantity and quality of research, what was studied, and the methods used. Finally, we look at the implication of the trends, the needs revealed by the trends, and some projections.

The data base for this analysis was provided by the former

119

ERIC Clearinghouse on Adult Education at Syracuse University and other sources reported in the literature. Because few investigators have examined the dissertation research in the field of adult education, this analysis is necessarily limited to those sometimes incomplete and inconsistent sources. However, the limitations do not appear to be so great as to detract significantly from the conclusions that may be drawn from the data.

The first dissertations in adult education were completed by Hallenback and Stacy in 1935. Since that date many graduate programs in adult education have emerged. Each program has extended the potential for quality and quantity in graduate research. As a result, there has been a dramatic increase in the volume of research, but what about quality?

Quality

Analyses of dissertations in adult education have led to the conclusion that the quality of graduate research is improving. Because of the close relationship between graduate research and research conducted by professors and others, graduate research generally reflects the quality of the research conducted by those persons. Consequently, the observation of Brunner and his coauthors (1959) that adult education was in a chaotic situation, with a strong emphasis on descriptive studies, described graduate research as well. The chaos seemed to mirror the developmental state of adult education as a field. At the time, there were two dozen or fewer professors of adult education, and the higher education dimension of adult education was only beginning to emerge. Thus, professors and students were working in an environment that placed a premium on activities that were somewhat different from contemporary goals.

Several factors contribute to the conclusion that the quality of graduate research is improving, even though it is difficult to determine or identify from the literature any criteria that outline what quality is. The first factor is the judgment of those who have analyzed the literature. Statements issued by some of these scholars are reported below. The second factor is the design element. Many of the more recent dissertations reflect an increasing sensitivity to, and awareness of, methods of research design that strengthen internal and external validity. Design also includes a third factor, knowledge of statistical analysis. A fourth, and very important, factor is the emerging concern for improved theoretical structures. As Boyd notes in Chapter Seven, much of the early survey research appears to have been conducted with only limited attention to broad theoretical frameworks. The more recent works are somewhat different in this respect.

The change in the broader field of adult education is reflected in DeCrow's conclusion (1966) that followed Brunner's by seven years. DeCrow noted that the quality and quantity of research had increased dramatically. His view is supported by Copeland and Grabowski, who reported "that the improvement of both the quality and quantity of adult education research continues" (1971, p. 23). This opinion was also expressed by DeCrow and Loague, who in their work at the Adult Education Clearinghouse closely scrutinized the flow of adult educators' dissertations: "We have an unmistakable impression of improved quality over the years, not only in the rigor of research procedures but also in the significance of the problems researched. Particularly, we feel that this improvement has extended down to master's degree research. ERIC/AE coverage of master's theses and papers is sporadic and highly dependent on submission of copies by the students or their professors. From the general sample we do see, however, the impression of improved quality and volume is quite definite and we expect that this research training of large numbers accounts, in part, for the great increase in recent years of well-contrived action research reports emanating from research and development projects out in the field" (1970, p. 15).

Quantity

Perhaps an easier change to observe and document is the volume of research. Before we pursue this topic, however, I want to point out certain limitations and definitions. First of all, this discussion is limited to dissertations; I omitted master's theses because they are not readily accessible. In addition, I have defined doctoral dissertations broadly to include all dissertations dealing with adult education, regardless of the university department from which they originated. And finally, two sources have been used, and these two sources do not always agree for a number of reasons; moreover, both may be incomplete. The first source is the list of graduates with doctoral degrees in adult education maintained at the University of Chicago. The second source, as I pointed out above, is the collection of abstracts at the ERIC Clearinghouse on Adult Education.

The criteria for inclusion in the University of Chicago list are these: "First, at the time the student did his work on the doctorate, he believed adult education to be his major field of specialization. Second, at the time the student did his work on the doctorate, the institution itself believed him to be securing his degree with a major specialization in adult education" (Houle and Buskey, 1966, p. 132). The University of Chicago records list 1713 adult education doctorates that were awarded between 1935 and 1975 (Houle and Ford, 1976, p. 63). On a year-to-year basis, the forties generally were characterized by fewer than 10 dissertations annually, the fifties by fewer than 30, and 1960 through 1968 by fewer than 70 each year. However, beginning in 1969 more than 100 dissertations were reported each year; 157 were reported just for 1975. The collection of dissertation abstracts developed by the ERIC Clearinghouse, even though not identical to the list maintained at the University of Chicago, reveals a similar trend.

Topics

What do these graduate students study? My analysis of what has been studied is based on the ERIC listing of 2150 dissertations rather than the Chicago list, because the ERIC collection provides more information. In the ERIC compilations, each dissertation was placed in a generic category accoding to its subject classification. This method of determining what the dissertation writers studied is somewhat limited and likely to oversimplify, but it does provide some broad indication of their interests. The editors of the various compilations recognized that many studies were pertinent to several subjects but had to decide into which one category each dissertation best fitted. Whatever arbitrary decisions the editors made in this regard were consistent throughout the three volumes (DeCrow and Loague, 1970; Grabowski, 1973; Grabowski and Loague, 1970).

An examination of the three volumes shows that in terms of numbers and broad categories, "program areas of adult education" and "institutional sponsors" were the most popular. Among more specific categories, several showed high activity: adult basic education; management development and supervisory education; occupational training of unskilled and disadvantaged adults; home, family, and parent education; human relations and laboratory training; cooperative and rural extension; and psychological and personality variables. The editors of the 1968–69 compilation suggested that federal legislation seemed to be the factor most responsible for the high rate of productivity in some of the categories. They pointed out that "five new laws seem to have played an important role in the new orientation: the Manpower Development and Training Act (MDTA) of 1962, the Vocational Education Act of 1963, the Economic Opportunity Act of 1964, Title I of the Higher Education Act of 1965, and the Adult Education Act of 1966" (Grabowski and Loague, 1970, p. 11).

Continuing education in technical and professional fields, with 58 dissertations, was the specific category with the largest number of dissertations completed between 1963 and 1969. Of these, 18 concerned medicine and health, and the remaining 40 dealt with engineering and architecture, education, law, religion, public administration, social work, technical education, and various other professions. The next largest specific category was agriculture and home economics, on which 48 dissertations were completed between 1963 and 1969. Most of these dissertations related to the Cooperative Extension Service and covered such topics as the adoption of innovative practices, farm management, the analysis of training needs, and the education of home economists. A dramatic decrease occurred in the number of dissertations completed in three other specific categories between 1963 and 1969 as compared with 1935 to 1962: psychological and personality variables dropped from 115 to 15; home, family, and parent education dropped from 112 to 17; and religious organizations dropped from 66 to 14.

Choosing the Topic. How and why graduate students select

the particular subjects of their dissertations has been a point of discussion for some time among both students and professors. For example, DeCrow and Loague observed: [The] "known research predilections of famous professors can very faintly be discovered in some cases. Some universities have more clear-cut interest patterns, but they are less definite than expected. It is apparent, even in this period, that the interests of 'extension' training programs and the more general degree programs are rapidly merging. We think that the personal interests and vocational initiative of the students themselves largely guide the choice of dissertation topics" (1970, p. 9). These observations were borne out in a survey of the members of the Commission of Professors conducted by Thorson (1973) to determine their attitudes toward research for the doctoral dissertation. Thorson found that the professors felt that students, as a group, had freedom to choose their own research topic and that students were encouraged to exercise that freedom (p. 8). However, some professors, in response to Thorson's questions about students' freedom to select their topic and their research methods, wrote in comments, such as, "I want my students to have freedom, but I also want them to work within my area of competence," and "I direct students to other professors if they select a problem outside my field" (p. 9).

However free students are to choose, one can observe some general patterns in their interests and motivations. "The distribution of subjects studied seems to reflect the three basic concerns which draw persons to a long-term, professional interest in adult education: (1) interest in some particular group of adults being served or in a program area; (2) concern with organizing, developing, supporting, and administering the work of a particular sponsoring agency; (3) interest in building or transmitting the knowledge base which supports the profession" (DeCrow and Loague, 1970, p. 9).

Neglected Topics. Some subjects have received a great deal of attention; others have clearly been neglected. Among the latter are educational materials, devices, and facilities; the occupational training of adults in business and industry; labor education; need-determination processes; counseling; alternative systems of education throughout the lifespan; instructional techniques; new careers; and paraprofessions (although interest in these subjects has been increasing since the last summary listing was published). Some of these topics were included by Knowles in his list of gaps in knowledge about the teaching of adults. In answer to a question he put to himself, "What research do I need to help me improve as a teacher?" he outlined the following categories (1972, pp. 272, 302):

1. Conceptualizing better role performance models for the adult educator.
2. The developmental processes of the adult educator.
3. Changes in the perceptual structures, perceptual modes, and perceptual habits of adults.
4. The learning sets that adults bring into the educational transaction.
5. Better understanding of the environmental forces that influence learning.
6. How to help adults diagnose their own needs for learning.
7. Better methodological theory.
8. Design theory.
9. The transfer of learning.
10. Articulation between childhood, youth, and adult learning.

Methods

Another important consideration, in addition to what the dissertation writers studied, is the methods they used. The editors of the last two ERIC compilations, covering the years 1963–67 and 1968–69, prepared "methodological indexes" showing under each subject heading in the volumes the number of studies that had been done using each of five types of research: experimental, descriptive, historical, methodological, and philosophical. The editors relied on the research definitions of Kerlinger (1967) and Mouly (1963) in classifying the dissertations. According to Kerlinger (1964, pp. 700–701), "methodological research is controlled investigation of the theoretical and applied aspects of measurement, mathematics and statistics, and ways of obtaining and analyzing data."

Most of the dissertations (70 percent) from 1963 through 1969 were descriptive, bearing out Brunner and others' observation (1959) about research in nonvocational adult education. DeCrow and Loague (1970, p. 13), commenting on the 1963–67 *Adult Education Dissertation Abstracts* compilation, noted: "Given the sprawl of adult education across almost every institution of American life and its constant penetration to new audiences in new programs by new methods, research done by individuals working largely with their own resources is likely to be of this type. Overwhelmingly, these are 'surveys' of the characteristics, participation patterns, attitudes, or educational needs of various agencies or locations; of the use of various methods; and of administrative practices. Many of these studies use national samples; most of them are rigorous enough in execution that valid generalizations can be made from them."

Although descriptive studies continue to predominate, the overall trend in methodological matters is toward greater sophistication. For instance, Copeland and Grabowski pointed out in 1971 (p. 24) that "more research studies are formulated within a theoretical framework. The quality of descriptive studies has been enhanced with the development of more powerful statistical tests (namely, techniques for multivariate analysis) and computer programs." They go on to add, "Two diametrically opposed trends seem to be developing. On the one hand, more rigor is evident in the empirical and experimental research. More attention is now given to the theoretical framework, the sampling design, the instrumentation, and the analysis of the data. On the other hand, there is increasing interest in and use of methods, such as participant-observer and futures-casting methods, that provide data other than what are considered 'hard data' " (p. 27).

Knowles (1973) has developed a conception of the developmental needs for research in a field of social practice in which he has set forth six organic needs and matched each one with several research methods he considered relevant to these needs. Looking at Knowles' schema (p. 302) and the kinds of methods used by dissertation writers in adult education, one can say that more attention ought to be given at least to the following: philosophical methods, historical analyses, analytical case studies, action research, and interdisciplinary and comparative studies. These approaches are particularly appropriate in the light of some remarks Ruddock (1972) made about statistical research. Although he wrote about the situation in England, his criticisms apply equally to graduate research in the United States and Canada. Ruddock conceded "that measurement has a certain short-run administrative utility," but he argued that "the naive approach that identified research with measurement has been particularly damaging." He maintained that "the great issues are bound up with philosophic, religious, theological, social and political systems," and these "great issues escape measurement, and have in consequence been neglected." He suggested that students "be invited to view their proposals in relation to major issues and possibly to wider theoretical and methodological perspectives" (1972, p. 60).

In an attempt to identify the main sources of research from which he received help as a teacher of adults, Knowles listed eight categories, then made this observation: "Now, as I look at these . . . , a couple of observations strike me. One is the virtual absence of quantitative research in that list. The people who have influenced me are not primarily numbers counters. They are not Chi-square testers. Two-tailed T tests are not central to their vocabulary—even analysis of variance, with or without regression formulas. It impresses me, now that I think about it, that the chief insights about the art of teaching have come from people who have looked at the human being as a gestalt—a unified, evolving, breathing, aspiring, needing, wanting, dynamic organism. To them, an insight—empirically tested—is a research finding" (1972, p. 272). And Knowles (1972) lends strong support to Ruddock from the standpoint of a teacher of adults.

In summary, the trend in dissertation research seems to indicate that students are giving less attention to topics previously covered extensively and are more concerned with newer areas of interest. Much of the new focus has been prompted by new laws funding various projects. Changes in topics have been accompanied by changes in the methods. Predominantly descriptive research has given way to experimental and methodological types of research with a smattering of historical and philosophical types, all of which indicate the increasing sophistication and maturity of the research element of graduate programs in adult education.

The Future

Graduate research is taking on a new look. As adult education becomes better established and recognized by other disciplines as a distinct field of study, much of the previous defensiveness expressed in a need to prove itself as a profession has given way to self-assurance. Such security should encourage more sophisticated methods and allow for hard critical assessment of its progress.

Adult education, drawing as it does from related disciplines such as anthropology, psychology, sociology, and even economics, political science, and history, must always share research endeavors with these fields. This limitation, if it be one, is also the glory and strength of adult education research even on the graduate level. For example, evaluation, continuing professional education, and the future of adult education in degree and credential programs are subjects in which adult education and other disciplines have a mutual interest and about which they ought to pursue research both independently and jointly. However, one would hope that graduate researchers would also address the needs of practitioners—needs such as those expressed by Knowles (1972)—particularly when one considers that adult education is a helping profession or one of social practice, as Knowles refers to it.

Another kind of research that needs to be done more is the longitudinal study. Ordinarily, a doctoral student will undertake a relatively small study which he can complete within a reasonable period of time in order to obtain a union card. Why not have a continuous study undertaken by one university's adult education department to which doctoral students can contribute one sequential segment? All the present purpose of a doctoral dissertation would still be served, and in addition some significant contributions on a large scale could be made to the field.

Graduate research in adult education is evolving from a primitive effort to an "advanced" endeavor, as the growing numbers of professors and graduate students alike show increasing sophistication in the use of advanced research methods. Surely adult education has matured since the time when it was regarded as an emerging field of university study; now, theory, practice, and training are advancing on an ever-widening and deepening front.

Epilogue

Roger Hiemstra
Huey B. Long

Developments in the education of adults are obviously occurring with increasing rapidity. The rate of increase, however, may normally go unnoticed unless one is fortunate enough to be engaged in a continuing review of the field. Such a review was required of the editors of this volume, and consequently we could not help but be aware of the growing attention being given to studies and investigations into topics related to the education of adults. Because of this intensification, we think an epilogue is desirable to note the research heritage of adult education, the emerging theoretical foundations, and some observations concerning future directions.

The authors of the eight chapters preceding this one outline a number of ideas, methods, and trends in adult education. Indeed, the fact that this publication is a separate volume in a new adult education handbook series reveals that research in the field has achieved a high level of development in comparison to that reflected in the first handbook. In reaching this level, the field has built up a rich store of research. Of course, we cannot capture in a short concluding chapter all the appropriate contributing publications, researchers, theorists, and efforts. But we can note some of the contributions for the reader's further study and reflection.

The overview work of Brunner and others (1959) certainly did much to establish an important foundation for understanding the research findings and needs of adult education. Similar efforts on a smaller scale can be found as special chapters in past handbooks on adult education. In this same manner, the work of Jensen (1964) in pointing out the field's reformulating endeavors and the other chapter contributors in that same book provided an important benchmark. In addition, as Grabowski pointed out in Chapter Eight of the present book, several efforts by ERIC personnel and by Houle and his associates at the University of Chicago have been made in the past decade to identify research activity, trends, and findings in adult education, primarily those by or concerning graduate students. And various adult education authors have done some special work to highlight research needs or to build a foundation for carrying out adult education research (Apps, 1972; Knowles, 1973; Kreitlow, 1968, 1975; Mezirow, 1971). Another means by which some researchers have contributed to an understanding of adult education has been through an analysis of the research activity itself. Grabowski in Chapter Eight summarizes and extends many of these efforts. The writings of Dickinson and Rusnell (1971), Long (1977), and Long and Agyekum (1974) are also noteworthy in this respect. Our final observation regarding adult education's research heritage is this: Most of the research, perhaps with the exception of studies of adult learning, has been carried out by graduate students and professors of adult education. And certainly much future research on this field will be carried out by the same two groups. But the examination of adult education must become a very broad, comprehensive enterprise. People in government bureaus, practitioners in a variety of operating agencies, employees in special research institutions, private researchers, and university researchers in a variety of disciplines must be encouraged to do more research on adult education problems, topics, and issues. This book may help facilitate such activity.

Theoretical Foundations

It may be premature, and indeed some would consider it presumptive, to suggest that definitive theoretical foundations now underpin the development of curriculum, programs, and teaching approaches in adult education. However, as will be shown in the other volumes in the Handbook Series, a great deal is now known about the field of adult education. And research in adult education has undoubtedly contributed to several emerging theories. The purpose of this section is to point out several of these theories about which a considerable body of knowledge has been gathered.

Three recent publications have examined research in adult education across a wide front. Utilizing primarily the journal *Adult Education* as a frame of reference, Hiemstra (1976, pp. 84–94) identified several topics on which considerable research information exists and about which, in many cases, conclusions of a theoretical nature have been drawn: the participant, dropping out and persevering, intelligence and achievement, learning and psychology, methods and media, program planning and administration, and teachers of adults. In addition, he cited two subjects—andragogy and the adult's projects (self-directed learning)—on which theories are evolving and suggested that additional research is required to more clearly understand them.

Another publication devoted to identifying cohesive research findings is by Knox (1977). Although focusing primarily on what he calls "systematic learning by adults," Knox divides his material into three broad categories and several subcategories (pp. 6–32): (1) adults as learners: learning, personality, performance, condition, context; (2) program development: setting, needs, objectives, activities, evaluation; and (3) organization and administration: participation, staffing, resources, organization, leadership, perspective. An attractive feature of the Knox work is his pinpointing of gaps in existing knowledge, his detailing of many promising research questions related to his theory categories, and his suggestions for new directions in research.

The third recent publication (College Entrance Examination Board, 1978) describes four basic subjects of research that should be given priority in the College Board's "Future Directions for a Learning Society" program.

1. Research that focuses primarily on learners
   A. The needs of learners that may be met through lifelong learning

    B. The characteristics or conditions that facilitate or impede adults' engaging in and benefiting from learning opportunities
2. Research that focuses primarily on providers
    A. The characteristics or conditions of institutional and individual providers that may influence adults' participating in and benefiting from learning activities
    B. The administrative and management functions of provider institutions that either facilitate or impede the provision of learning opportunities
3. Research that focuses primarily on society, especially on the impact of lifelong learning
4. Research that focuses on the interactions of learners, providers, and society
    A. The ways in which providers and learners interact to facilitate lifelong learning
    B. The impact of society on learners; public policies and practices that facilitate or impede adult learning
    C. The impact of society (public practices and policies) on providers of learning opportunities
    D. The dissemination and use of research findings

    These three lists illustrate both the diverse and common interests in adult-education research. Though the concepts focused on in the three lists differ, the generic elements reveal considerable overlap. Communication concerning the generic elements, however, is confounded and complicated by the lack of a widely accepted standard terminology and by the conceptual variance in research. These conditions present a significant challenge to those who are trying to advance theory by devising research strategies and setting priorities for research activities.

Future Directions

    Although the specific directions of research and procedures may be difficult to forecast, it is not difficult to identify several interrelated factors that will stimulate research activity. The increasing number of adults engaging in all kinds of educative activities and the concomitant growing efforts of numerous providers to attract and serve adults will exert pressure for government support of such activities. Consequently, the need for better understanding and knowledge of adult learning and related topics will become more urgent. And this urgency will likely generate additional pressures and incentives for diverse research efforts. Thus, we predict that research activity will increase. Furthermore, researchers will probably continue to expand on the range of topics discussed in the first eight chapters of this book, including the topics mentioned in the preceding section of this chapter.

Clearly, research in adult education is constantly deepening and broadening. Not only has research been increasing in both diversity and amount, it is also becoming more sophisticated. As Carlson, Darkenwald, Dickinson and Blunt, and Grabowski point out in earlier chapters, a great deal of research, descriptive or historical in nature, continues to be needed and carried out. And more and more adult education researchers are asking the hard question why, in addition to what, where and when. A greater attention to method and design, a wise use of experimental designs, manipulation and analysis of multiple variables, analytical efforts based on the capacities of the computer, and the increased involvement of adult educators in annual research-related seminars or conferences are some of the very promising signs of maturation and theory development. Indeed, experienced adult educators who have been professionally engaged in the field long enough to have developed some historical perspective can look with some satisfaction on the growing maturity of the field in terms of its research.

We further predict that this development will continue, because of increased social attention to adult education and lifelong learning, greater need for continued learning, and the "discovery" of the adult as a learner by many institutions of higher education. The consequent involvement of researchers in such specialized fields as educational gerontology and adult counseling, the improving research skill of professionals coming from graduate programs of adult education, and the growing effectiveness of many new clearinghouse organizations should foster this growth. A future edition of this volume almost certainly will reveal much more about the methods, content, and impact of adult education research than can now be expressed.

Future discussions of research and investigations into the phenomena of adult learning will more fully reveal how the methods of describing, measuring, and interpreting such phenomena have developed even while this book was in progress. As each of the preceding chapters has revealed, almost every kind of research method is the subject of continuing critical review.

The methods discussed in this volume reflect the traditional types of research subsumed under qualitative and quantitative labels. Research on adult education phenomena has included techniques of observation, testing, and statistical analysis in a variety of forms. However, investigators have also employed more qualitative methods, as recommended by Apps (1972) and by Darkenwald in this book. These methods include participant observation, in-depth interviewing, full participation in the processes being examined, fieldwork, and related activities. As a result, the disciplined qualitative approach leads to careful descriptions of what goes on in given situations. Descriptions so generated are rich in detail and interpretation and aid the investigator in seeking to understand causality without the need to dissect reality into its component parts.

The other side of the issue is represented by Long's chapter on the experimental method, in which he seeks to encourage mutual appreciation by investigators from both the qualitative and the quantitative schools. Quantitatively oriented investigators need to realize that a single observation of the occurrence of a phenomenon is sufficient to prove that the phenomenon is possible. Concomitantly, qualitatively oriented researchers should recognize that their data are usually insufficient to establish the degree to which the observed phenomenon is probable. Probability can be established only by analyzing how often the phenomenon occurs in a sample of observations. Such analysis is not possible without enumeration, sampling, precise measurement, and statistical treatment.

Long's comments in Chapter Six suggested that adult education research is on the brink of discovering or employing what has been called the descriptive-correlational-experimental loop. This paradigm contains three fundamental elements: the development of ways to describe phenomena in a quantitative manner; the employment of correlational studies in which the descriptive variables are related to selected dependent variables; and the use of experimental studies in which the critical variables identified in the correlational studies are tested in a controlled environment. We know that the first two fundamental elements in this loop are present in adult education research in many studies. Therefore, we may logically expect future research to reveal the third element, providing the quality of the first two elements is sufficient to enable us to identify the appropriate critical variables for controlled experimentation.

Somewhere between the most conservative proponents of either the qualitative or the quantitative research philosophy we find a number of moderates, who are likely to combine the strength of both approaches by using intensive experimental designs. In such a design the researcher substitutes frequency of observation for numbers of subjects; he studies one or a few individuals or phenomena but conducts repeated observations of the single case before, during, and after some experimental treatment. Boshier's study (1975) of the use of operant conditioning in an adult education course is an example of this procedure.

At the other end of the methodological spectrum is the method of path analysis. Though the literature does not reveal great quantities of outstanding research in this mode, a number of dissertations appear to be based on model-building activities that are frequently related to path analysis. Path analysis begins with a model that represents the variables that are considered to be involved in contributing to variance in a specific outcome, such as adults' achievement in basic education. Using this procedure, the researcher arranges the variables in what is judged to be, on external or a priori grounds, a causal sequence. For example, if the ability to count precedes another variable such as the ability to add, the ability to count is posited as a cause of (or contributor to) the ability to do addition. Generally, chronological sequence affects assumptions about causal sequence. Evidence from previous correlational and experimental research can also serve as a basis for causal inferences.

This epilogue expresses a basically optimistic view of the prospects for research. Previous research, conducted during the infancy and adolescence of adult education as a field, has not been altogether barren of significant results. And the comments in other chapters and in the preceding sections of this epilogue present a number of promising ideas about ways to enhance the next round of research effort. Reviews of histories and philosophies of science, technology, and medicine reveal that progress in these fields has frequently occurred in spurts based on long periods of apparently fruitless basic investigations. For example, in the 1930s most medical writers could have complained about the apparent therapeutic fruitlessness of research on microbes and related disease factors over the previous half century. There was then no cure for lobar pneumonia, syphilis, typhoid, and a number of other microbial diseases. But forty years later, a hundred-year view shows that significant and necessary basic research was done during that so-called fruitless first half century.

Similarly, the prospect that lies before adult education research is one of more definitive and effective knowledge gradually emerging from the efforts made in our first fifty years. The prospect suggests that adult education investigators will follow the descriptive-correlational-experimental paradigm and clean up a number of unfinished details. Fresh and novel variables will be identified, conceptualized, and measured. More resourceful ways of casting the interrelationships of variables will be invented and exploited. Improved qualitative studies, more comprehensive and more sophisticated correlational studies, additional intensive and single-case experiments, and more path analyses are likely. Such potential developments, however, do not necessarily imply that a unitary concept of research will characterize most investigations.

Even in the unlikely event of consensus concerning a specific research method, disagreement will probably continue on the focus of the research: applied or basic. Traditionally, scientific achievements are pluralistic in nature; some are serendipitous and others result from a specific planned attack on a practical problem. Penicillin is a classical illustration of the former, and the atomic bomb illustrates the latter. Thus, we may contemplate the possibility that advances in adult education will come about in similar ways. Some may grow out of research results in such fields as physiology, chemistry, microbiology, statistics, and computer science. Others will occur as a result of direct attempts to answer such questions as, What is the best way to teach a specific topic to a specific learner? Or, what is (are) the best way(s) to attract a specific learner to a specific educational activity and keep the learner there? Both kinds of research are required if professionals and volunteers in adult education are to improve service and instruction for adult learners of all kinds.

References

ADAMS, R., AND PREISS, J. (Eds.). *Human Organization Research.* Homewood, Ill.: Dorsey, 1960.

AKER, G. F. "The Identification of Criteria for Evaluating Graduate Programs in Adult Education." Unpublished doctoral dissertation, University of Wisconsin, 1962.

AKER, G. F., AND SCHROEDER, W. L. "Research for Action Programs." In N. C. Shaw (Ed.), *Administration of Continuing Education.* Washington, D.C.: National Association for Public School Education, 1969.

ALLERTON, T. D. "Characteristics of the Learning Projects Pursued by Selected Seminary-Educated Parish Ministers Serving in the Metropolitan Louisville Area." Unpublished doctoral dissertation, University of Georgia, 1974.

AMERICAN PSYCHOLOGICAL ASSOCIATION. *Publication Manual of the American Psychological Association.* (2nd ed.) Washington, D.C.: American Psychological Association, 1974.

ANDREWS, F., AND OTHERS. *A Guide for Selecting Statistical Techniques for Analyzing Social Science Data.* Ann Arbor: Institute for Social Research, Survey Research Center, University of Michigan, n.d.

APPS, J. W. "Toward a Broader Definition of Research." *Adult Education,* 1972, *23,* 59–64.

AUSUBEL, D. *Educational Psychology: A Cognitive View.* New York: Holt, Rinehart and Winston, 1968.

BARITZ, L. "The Historian as Playwright." *The Nation,* November 24, 1962, pp. 340–343.

BEALS, R., AND BRODY, L. *The Literature of Adult Education.* New York: American Association for Adult Education, 1941.

BECKER, E. *The Revolution in Psychiatry.* New York: Free Press, 1964.

BEDER, H. W. "Community Linkages in Urban Public School Adult Basic Education Programs: A Study of Cosponsorship and the Use of Community Liaison Personnel." Unpublished doctoral dissertation, Columbia University, 1972.

BEDER, H. W., AND DARKENWALD, G. G. "Approaches to Upgrading Approved Research in Adult Education." Paper presented at Adult Education Research Conference, Chicago, April 1974.

BERGER, J., AND OTHERS. *Types of Formalization in Small-Group Research.* Boston: Houghton Mifflin, 1962.

BITTNER, W. S. "Adult Education." In W. S. Monroe (Ed.), *Encyclopedia of Educational Research.* (Rev. ed.) New York: Macmillan, 1950.

BLAKELY, R. J. *The New Environment: Questions for Adult Educators.* Occasional Papers, No. 23. Syracuse, N.Y.: Publications in Continuing Education, 1971.

BLEDSOE, J. C. *Essentials of Educational Research.* (2nd ed.) Athens, Ga.: Optima House, 1972.

BLOOM, B. S., AND OTHERS *Taxonomy of Educational Objectives: The Classification of Educational Goals.* New York: Longmans, Green, 1956.

BLUMER, H. *Symbolic Interactionism.* Englewood Cliffs, N.J.: Prentice-Hall, 1969.

BODENHAMER, S. H. "A Study of the Effects of Presenting Informative Speeches With and Without the Use of Visual Aids to Voluntary Adult Audiences." Unpublished doctoral dissertation, Ohio State University, 1964.

BORGATTA, E. F., AND BOHRNSTEDT, G. W. (Eds.). *Sociological Methodology 1970.* San Francisco: Jossey-Bass, 1970.

BOSHIER, R. "Motivational Orientations of Adult Education Participants: A Factor Analysis of Houle's Typology." *Adult Education,* 1971, *21,* 3–26.

Boshier, R. "Behavior Modification and Contingency Management in a Graduate Adult Education Program." *Adult Education*, 1975, *26* (1), 16–31.

Boyd, R. D. "New Designs for Adult Education Research Programs." *Adult Education*, 1969, *19*, 186–196.

Briggs, A. "The Social Sciences and History." In R. M. Hutchins and M. J. Adler (Eds.), *The Great Ideas Today*. New York: Praeger, 1966.

Bromley, D. B. "An Approach to Theory Construction in Psychology of Development and Aging." In L. R. Goulet and P. B. Baltes (Eds.), *Life-Span Developmental Psychology: Research and Theory*. New York: Academic Press, 1970.

Bruner, J., Goodnow, J., and Austin, G. *A Study of Thinking*. New York: Wiley, 1962.

Brunner, E. deS., and Others. *An Overview of Adult Education Research*. Chicago: Adult Education Association of the U.S.A., 1959.

Bryson, L. L. *Adult Education*. New York: American Book, 1936.

Buckholdt, D. R., and Ferriton, D. E. "Effect of Token Reinforcement on Two Attending Behaviors of Adults in a Continuing Education Program." *Adult Education*, 1974, 24 (3), 208–219.

Buros, O. K. *The Seventh Mental Measurement Yearbook*, Vols. 1 and 2. Highland Park, N.J.: Gryphon Press, 1972.

Campbell, D. T., and Stanley, J. C. *Experimental and Quasi-Experimental Designs for Research*. Chicago: Rand McNally, 1963.

Carlson, R. A. "Americanization as an Early Twentieth Century Adult Education Movement." *History of Education Quarterly*, 1970, *10*, 440–464.

Carlson, R. A. "Professional Leadership Versus The Educational Service Station Approach: An Historical Appraisal." *Adult Education*, 1972, *22*, 291–299.

Carpenter, W. L. "The Relationship Between Age and Information Processing Capacity and Age and Channel Capacity of Adults." Unpublished doctoral dissertation, Florida State University, 1967.

Carr, E. H. *What Is History?* New York: Knopf, 1965.

Chambers, M. M. "Selection, Definition and Delimitation of a

Doctoral Research Problem." *Phi Delta Kappan*, 1960, *53*, 71–73.

CLARK, B. R. *Adult Education in Transition*. Berkeley: University of California Press, 1968.

COHEN, M. R., AND NAGEL, E. *An Introduction to Logic and Scientific Method*. New York: Harcourt Brace Jovanovich, 1934.

COLE, J. W., JR., AND GLASS, J. C., JR. "The Effects of Adult Student Participation in Program Planning on Achievement, Retention and Attitude." *Adult Education*, 1977, *27* (2), 75–88.

COLLEGE ENTRANCE EXAMINATION BOARD. *"Lifelong Learning During Adulthood: An Agenda for Research."* New York: College Entrance Examination Board, 1978.

COLLINS, M. "The Mechanics' Institutes of the U.K.: A Study of Middle-Class Dominance Within a National Movement in Adult Education." Unpublished master's thesis, University of Saskatchewan, 1969.

COLLINS, M. "The Mechanics' Institute—Education for the Working Man?" *Adult Education*, 1972, *23*, 37–47.

COMMISSION OF THE PROFESSORS OF ADULT EDUCATION. *Adult Education: A New Imperative for Our Times*. Chicago: Adult Education Association of the U.S.A., 1961.

CONANT, J. B. *On Understanding Science*. New Haven, Conn.: Yale University Press, 1947.

COPELAND, H. G., AND GRABOWSKI, S. M. "Research and Investigation in the United States." *Convergence*, 1971, *4*, 23–32.

CORNELL, F. G., AND McLOORE, E. P. "Design of Sample Surveys in Education." *Review of Educational Research*, 1963, *33*, 523–532.

CRONBACH, L. J. *Essentials of Psychological Testing*. New York: Harper & Row, 1969.

DECROW, R. "New Directions in Adult Education Research." *Continuing Education for Adults*. Syracuse, N.Y.: University College, Syracuse University, 1966.

DECROW, R. "Research and Investigations in Adult Education." *Adult Education*, 1967, *17*, 195–258.

DECROW, R., AND LOAGUE, N. (Eds.). *Adult Education Dissertation Abstracts, 1963–1967*. Washington, D.C.: Adult Education Association of the U.S.A., 1970.

DEMING, W. E. "On Errors in Surveys." In N. K. Denzin (Compiler), *Sociological Methods: A Sourcebook*. Chicago: Aldine, 1970.

DENZIN, N. K. (Compiler). *The Research Act: A Theoretical Introduction to Sociological Methods*. Chicago: Aldine, 1970.

DEWEY, J., AND BENTLEY, A. *Knowing and the Known*. Boston: Beacon Press, 1949.

DICKINSON, G. "Educational Variables and Participation in Adult Education: An Exploratory Study." *Adult Education*, 1971, *22*, 36–47.

DICKINSON, G., AND RUSNELL, D. "A Content Analysis of *Adult Education.*" *Adult Education*, 1971, *21*, 177–185.

DOLAN, J. A. "Sean O'Casey: An Adult Educator." Unpublished master's thesis, University of Saskatchewan, 1972.

DOLLINS, C. N. "The Effect of Group Discussion Learning Procedure on the Adaptive Social Behavior of Educable Adult Mental Retardates." Unpublished doctoral dissertation, Indiana University, 1967.

DOUGLAH, M. A., AND MOSS, G. M. "Adult Education as a Field of Study and Its Implications for the Preparation of Adult Educators." *Adult Education*, 1969, *19*, 127–134.

DUBIN, R. *Theory Building*. New York: Free Press, 1969.

ERIKSON, E. H. *Childhood and Society*. New York: Norton, 1950.

ESSERT, P. "Adult Education: An Overview." *Review of Educational Research*, 1953, *23*, 195–201.

ETTER, D. C. G. "Adult Learner Characteristics and Instructional Objectives." Unpublished doctoral dissertation, University of California at Los Angeles, 1969.

FESTINGER, L., AND KATZ, D. *Research Methods in the Social Sciences*. New York: Dryden Press, 1953.

FILSTEAD, W. *Qualitative Methodology: Firsthand Involvement in the Social World*. Chicago: Markham, 1970.

FISHBEIN, M. (Ed.). *Readings in Attitude Theory and Measurement*. New York: Wiley, 1967.

FOREST, L. B. "Beyond Scientific Empiricism in Adult Education Research." Paper presented at Adult Education Research Conference, Chicago, April 1972.

FREIRE, P. *Pedagogy of the Oppressed*. New York: Herder and Herder, 1970.

FROMM, E. *The Revolution of Hope*. New York: Bantam Books, 1971.

GAGE, N. L. (Ed.). *Handbook of Research on Teaching*. Chicago: Rand McNally, 1962.

GAGE, N. L. *The Scientific Basis of The Art of Teaching*. New York: Teachers College Press, Columbia University, 1978.

GALJART, B. "Rural Development and Sociological Concepts: A Critique." *Rural Sociology*, 1971, *36*, 31–41.

GEPHART, W. J. *The Eight General Research Methodologies: A Facet Analysis of the Research Process*. Bloomington, Ind.: Phi Delta Kappa Research Service Center, 1969.

GEPHART, W. J. AND BARTOS, B. B. *Profiling Instructional Package*. Occasional Paper No. 7. Bloomington, Ind.: Phi Delta Kappa Research Service Center, 1969.

GLASER, R. "Cognitive Psychology and Instructional Design." In D. Klahr (Ed.), *Cognition and Instruction*. Hillsdale. N.J.: Erlbaum Associates, 1976.

GLASER, B. G., AND STRAUSS, A. L. *Awareness of Dying*. Chicago: Aldine, 1965.

GLASER, B. G., AND STRAUSS, A. L. *The Discovery of Grounded Theory*. Chicago: Aldine, 1967.

GLASS, G. V. "The Growth of Evaluation Methodology." A paper presented at Evaluation Workshop for Adult Education Research Conference, Minneapolis, March 1970.

GOTTSCHALK, L. *Understanding History: A Primer of Historical Method*. New York: Knopf, 1950.

GRABOWSKI, S. M. (Ed.). *Adult Education Dissertation Abstracts 1935–1962*. Washington, D.C.: Adult Education Association of the U.S.A., 1973.

GRABOWSKI, S. M., AND LOAGUE, N. (Eds.). *Adult Education Dissertation Abstracts, 1968–1969*. Washington, D.C.: Adult Education Association of the U.S.A., 1970.

GROTELUESCHEN, A. "Differentially Structured Introductory Learning Tasks." Unpublished doctoral dissertation, Columbia University, 1967.

GUETZKOW, H. "Unitizing and Categorizing Problems in Coding Qualitative Data." *Journal of Clinical Psychology*, 1950, *6*, 47–58.

HALLENBECK, W. C. "Conceptual Structure for Some Aspects of Adult Education." In G. E. Jensen, A. A. Liveright, and W. Hallenbeck (Eds.), *Adult Education: Outlines of an Emerging Field of University Study*. Chicago: Adult Education Association of the U.S.A., 1964.

HAMMOND, P. *Sociologists at Work*. New York: Basic Books, 1964.

HAVENS, A. E. "Methodological Issues in the Study of Development." *Sociologia Ruralis*, 1972, *12*, 252–272.

HENDRICKSON, A. "Adult Education." In C. W. Harris and M. R. Liba (Eds.), *Encyclopedia of Educational Research*. (3rd ed.) New York: Macmillan, 1960.

HIEMSTRA, R. *Lifelong Learning*. Lincoln, Nebr.: Professional Educators Publications, 1976.

HIGHAM, J. *History: The Development of Historical Studies in the United States*. Englewood Cliffs, N.J.: Prentice-Hall, 1965.

HILL, J. E., AND KERBER, A. *Models, Methods, and Analytical Procedures in Educational Research*. Detroit: Wayne State University Press, 1967.

HILLWAY, T. *Introduction to Research*. (2nd. ed.) Boston: Houghton Mifflin, 1974.

HOROWITZ, I. L. *The Rise and Fall of Project Camelot: Studies in the Relationship Between Social Science and Practical Politics*. Cambridge, Mass.: M.I.T. Press, 1967.

HOULE, C. O. "Other Developments." *Review of Educational Research*, 1953, *23*, 268–276.

HOULE, C. O. "The Educators of Adults." In R. M. Smith and others (Eds.), *Handbook of Adult Education*. New York: Macmillan, 1970.

HOULE, C. O. *The External Degree*. San Francisco: Jossey-Bass, 1973.

HOULE, C. O., AND BUSKEY, J. H. "The Doctorate in Adult Education, 1935–1965." *Adult Education,* 1966, *16*, 131–168.

HOULE, C. O., AND FORD, D. "1975 Doctorates in Adult Education." *Adult Leadership*, 1976, *25*, 63–64.

HUBER, J. "Symbolic Interaction as a Pragmatic Perspective: The

Bias of Emergent Theory." *American Sociological Review*, 1973, 274–284.

HUDSON, J. *The History of Adult Education*. London: Woburn Press, 1969. (Originally published 1851.)

IANNACCONE, L. "Interdisciplinary Theory Guided Research in Educational Administration: A Smoggy View from the Valley." *Teachers College Record*, 1973, *75*, 55–66.

ILLICH, I. *Deschooling Society*. New York: Harper & Row, 1971.

INHELDER, B., AND PIAGET, J. *The Growth of Logical Thinking from Childhood to Adolescence*. New York: Basic Books, 1958.

ISRAELI, E. "Comparative Analysis of Program Development Processes in Synagogue Adult Jewish Education." Unpublished doctoral dissertation, Columbia University, 1973.

JACKSON, P. W. *Life in Classrooms*. New York: Holt, Rinehart and Winston, 1968.

JENSEN, G. "How Adult Education Borrows and Reformulates Knowledge of Other Disciplines." In G. E. Jensen, A. A. Liveright, and W. Hallenbeck (Eds.), *Adult Education: Outlines of an Emerging Field of University Study*. Chicago: Adult Education Association of the U.S.A., 1964.

JOHNSTONE, J. W. C., AND RIVERA, R. J. *Volunteers for Learning: A Study of the Educational Pursuits of American Adults*. Chicago: Aldine, 1965.

KAPLAN, A. "Introduction to Research Review." *Adult Education*, 1957, *7*, 195–196.

KAUFMANN, H. *Introduction to the Study of Human Behavior*. Philadelphia: Saunders, 1968.

KERLINGER, F. N. *Foundations of Behavioral Research: Educational and Psychological Inquiry*. New York: Holt, Rinehart and Winston, 1964.

KERLINGER, F. N. *Foundations of Behavioral Research*. (2nd ed.) New York: Holt, Rinehart and Winston, 1973.

KISH, L. "Some Statistical Problems in Research Design." *American Sociological Review*, 1959, *24*, 328–338.

KISH, L. *Survey Sampling*. New York: Wiley, 1965.

KNOWLES, M. S. "The Relevance of Research for the Adult Education Teacher/Trainer." *Adult Leadership*, 1972, *20*, 270–272, 302.

KNOWLES, M. S. "Sequential Research Needs in Evolving Disciplines of Social Practice." *Adult Education*, 1973, *23*, 298–303.

KNOX, A. *Current Research Needs Related to Systematic Learning by Adults*. Occasional Paper No. 4. Urbana: Office for the Study of Continuing Professional Education, College of Education, University of Illinois at Urbana-Champaign, 1977.

KREITLOW, B. W. "Adult Education: An Overview." *Review of Educational Research*, 1959, *29*, 223–229.

KREITLOW, B. W. "Research in Adult Education." In M. S. Knowles (Ed.), *Handbook of Adult Education*. Chicago: Adult Education Association of the U.S.A., 1960.

KREITLOW, B. W. "Relating Adult Education to Other Disciplines." Unpublished monograph, University of Wisconsin, 1964a.

KREITLOW, B. W. "Needed Research." *Review of Educational Research*, 1964b, *35*, 240–245.

KREITLOW, B. W. *Educating the Adult Educator. Part 2: Taxonomy of Needed Research*. Theoretical Paper No. 13. Madison: Wisconsin Research and Development Center for Cognitive Learning, University of Wisconsin, 1968.

KREITLOW, B. W. "Research and Theory." In R. M. Smith, G. F. Aker, and J. R. Kidd (Eds.), *Handbook of Adult Education*. New York: Macmillan, 1970.

KREITLOW, B. W. "Federal Support to Adult Education: Boon or Boondoggle." *Adult Education*, 1975, *25*, 231–237.

KRONUS, C. L. "Patterns of Adult Library Use: A Regression and Path Analysis." *Adult Education*, 1973, *23*, 115–131.

LAKATOS, I., AND MUSGROVE, A. (Eds.). *Criticism and the Growth of Knowledge*. Cambridge, England: Cambridge University Press, 1970.

LAKE, D., MILES, M., AND EARLE, R., JR. (Eds.). *Measuring Human Behavior*. New York: Teachers College Press, 1973.

LAZARSFELD, P. F., AND OTHERS (Eds.). *Continuities in the Language of Social Research*. New York: Free Press, 1972.

LIEBOW, E. *Tally's Corner*. Boston: Little, Brown, 1967.

LINDZEY, G. (Ed.). *Handbook of Social Psychology*. (rev. ed.) Vols. 1 and 2. Reading, Mass.: Addison-Wesley, 1960.

LITCHFIELD, A. "The Measurement and Patterns of Participation in

Adult Education Activities." Unpublished doctoral dissertation, University of Chicago, 1965.

LIVERIGHT, A. A. "The Nature and Aims of Adult Education as a Field of Graduate Education." In G. E. Jensen, A. A. Liveright, and W. Hallenbeck (Eds.), *Adult Education: Outlines of an Emerging Field of University Study.* Chicago: Adult Education Association of the U.S.A., 1964.

LLOYD, A. S. "Freire, Conscientization, and Adult Education." *Adult Education,* 1972, *23*, 3–20.

LONDONER, C. A. "Sources of Educational Funds as Motivators for Participating in Adult Secondary Education." *Adult Education,* 1974, *25* (1), 47–63.

LONG, H. B. "A Summary Report: Adult Education Participants in Brevard County, Florida." *Adult Education,* 1967, *18* (1), 34–42.

LONG, H. B. "Publication Activity of Selected Professors in Adult Education." *Adult Education,* 1977, *27*, 173–186.

LONG, H. B., AND AGYEKUM, S. K. "Adult Education 1964–1973: Reflections of a Changing Discipline." *Adult Education,* 1974, *24*, 99–120.

LUPTON, D. E. "Differential Patient Response to Instruction, Counseling, and Dental Treatment." Unpublished doctoral dissertation, University of Chicago, 1967.

McCALL, G., AND SIMMONS, J. L. *Issues in Participant Observation.* Reading, Mass.: Addison-Wesley, 1969.

McGINNIS, P. S. "Murray Thomson: Prophetic Reformer in 'The Land of Smiles.'" Unpublished master's thesis, University of Saskatchewan, 1972.

McKEACHIE, W. J., AND KULIK, J. A. "Effective College Teaching." In F. N. Kerlinger (Ed.), *Review of Research in Education: 3.* Itasca, Ill.: Peacock, 1975.

MACNEIL, T. "The Involvement of Nonmembers in Action Programs of Voluntary Groups: An Exploratory Study with Implications for Adult Education." Unpublished doctoral dissertation, University of Wisconsin, 1970.

MAJURE, W. C. "Acquiring Parent Participation in an Early Childhood Education Model." Unpublished doctoral dissertation, University of Nebraska, 1972.

MALTZMAN, E. "An Investigation of Key-Tone Matching with Children and Adults." Unpublished doctoral dissertation, Boston University, 1964.

MANDLER, G. AND KESSEN, W. *The Language of Psychology*. New York: Wiley, 1959.

MEIERHENRY, W. C. "The Potential Relationship Between the Findings of Cognitive Style Research and Findings of Right and Left Brain Hemispheric Research." Paper presented at the Adult Education Research Conference, San Antonio, Texas, April 1978.

MEZIROW, J. "Toward a Theory of Practice." *Adult Education*, 1971, *21*, 135–147.

MEZIROW, J., DARKENWALD, G., AND KNOX, A. *Last Gamble on Education: Dynamics of Adult Basic Education*. Washington, D.C.: Adult Education Association of the U.S.A., 1975.

MOULY, G. J. *The Science of Educational Research*. New York: American Book Co., 1963.

NATIONAL CENTER FOR EDUCATION STATISTICS. *Participation in Adult Education, Final Report 1972*. Washington, D.C.: National Center for Education Statistics and Department of Health, Education, and Welfare, 1975.

OPPENHEIMER, R. "Analogy in Science." *American Psychologist*, 1956, *11*, 127–135.

PENNINGTON, F., AND GREEN, J. "Comparative Analysis of Program Development Processes in Six Professions." *Adult Education*, 1976, *27* (1), 13–23.

PETERS, J. M. "Effects of Internal-External Control on Learning and Participation in Occupational Education." Unpublished doctoral dissertation, North Carolina State University, 1968.

PHILLIPS, B. S. *Social Research: Strategy and Tactics*. New York: Macmillan, 1971.

PIAGET, J. *Psychology of Intelligence*. New York: Littlefield, Adams, 1960.

POPPER, K. *The Logic of Scientific Discovery*. New York: Harper & Row, 1959.

RAPAPORT, D. (Ed.). *Organization and Pathology of Thought*. New York: Columbia University Press, 1959.

REIMER, E. *School Is Dead: Alternatives in Education*. New York: Doubleday, 1972.

RHYNE, D. C. "Attitude Set, Group Learning, and Attitude Change." Unpublished doctoral dissertation, North Carolina State University, 1968.

ROGERS, C. R. "Toward a Science of the Person." In T. W. Wann (Ed.), *Behaviorism and Phenomenology*. Chicago: University of Chicago Press, 1964.

ROSENBERG, M. *The Logic of Survey Analysis*. New York: Basic Books, 1968.

ROYCE, J. R. *The Encapsulated Man*. New York: D. Van Nostrand, 1964.

RUDDOCK, R. *Sociological Perspectives on Adult Education*. Monograph 2. Manchester, England: Department of Adult Education, University of Manchester, 1972.

SCHATZMAN, L., AND STRAUSS, A. *Field Research*. Englewood Cliffs, N.J.: Prentice-Hall, 1973.

SCHLESINGER, A. "The Limits of Social Science." In E. N. Saveth (Ed.), *American History and the Social Sciences*. New York: Free Press, 1964.

SCHROEDER, W. L. "Adult Education Defined and Described." In R. M. Smith and others (Eds.), *Handbook of Adult Education*. New York: Macmillan, 1970.

SELLTIZ, C., AND OTHERS. *Research Methods in Social Relations*. New York: Holt, Rinehart and Winston, 1959.

SHAH, F. B. "The Relationship of Group Size and Divergent Thinking Among Adults." Unpublished doctoral dissertation, Florida State University, 1966.

SHERWOOD, M. *The Logic of Explanation in Psychoanalysis*. New York: Academic Press, 1969.

SHILLACE, R. "Theory and Research in Adult Education." Paper presented at Adult Education Research Conference, Montreal, April 1973.

SIEBER, S. D. "The Integration of Fieldwork and Survey Methods." *American Journal of Sociology*, 1973, 78, 1335–1359.

SPENCE, R. B. "Adult Education: An Overview." *Review of Educational Research*, 1950, 20, 165–170.

SPENCE, R. B. "Role of Research in Adult Education." *Adult Education*, 1953, 3, 69–76.

SPENCE, R. B. "What Is Adult Education?" *Adult Education*, 1955, 5, 131–145.

STAKE, R. E. "Generalizability of Program Evaluation: The Need for Limits." *Educational Products Report*, Feb. 1969.

STANLEY, J. C. "The Influence of Fisher's 'The Design of Experiments' on Educational Research Thirty Years Later." *American Educational Research Journal*, 1966, *3*, 223–229.

STANLEY, J. C. *Measurement in Today's Schools*. Englewood Cliffs, N.J.: Prentice-Hall, 1969.

STEPHENSON, W. *The Study of Behavior*. Chicago: University of Chicago Press, 1958.

STOGDILL, R. (Ed.). *The Process of Model-Building in the Behavioral Sciences*. New York: Norton, 1970.

STROUP, H. "Checking the Learning Interests of Board Members." *Adult Education*, 1960, *11*, 12–13.

STRUNK, W., JR., AND WHITE, E. B. *The Elements of Style*. New York: Macmillan, 1965.

TAYLOR, A. J. P. *English History, 1914–1945*. Oxford, England: Clarendon Press, 1965.

THIEDE, W. B., AND DRAPER, J. "Research and Investigations in Adult Education." *Adult Education*, 1963, *13*, 195–216.

THIEDE, W. B., AND DRAPER, J. "Research and Investigations in Adult Education." *Adult Education*, 1964, *14*, 195–225.

THIEDE, W. B., AND MEGGARS, J. "Research and Investigations in Adult Education." *Adult Education*, 1965, *15*, 195–234.

THIEDE, W. B., AND MEGGARS, J. "Research and Investigations in Adult Education." *Adult Education*, 1966, *16*, 195–238.

THORNDIKE, E. L., AND OTHERS. *Adult Learning*. New York: Macmillan, 1928.

THORNDIKE, R. L. (Ed.). *Educational Measurement*. Washington, D.C.: American Council on Education, 1971.

THORSON, J. A. "Expressed Attitudes Toward the Doctoral Dissertation Among Adult Educators." Paper presented at Adult Education Research Conference, Montreal, April 1973.

TOFFLER, A. *Future Shock*. New York: Random House, 1970.

TOUGH, A. *The Adult's Learning Projects*. Ontario, Canada: Ontario Institute for Studies in Education, 1971.

TRAVERS, R. M. W. *An Introduction to Educational Research*. New York: Macmillan, 1964.

TROW, M. "Education and Survey Research." In C. Y. Gloch

(Ed.), *Survey Research in the Social Sciences.* New York: Russell Sage Foundation, 1967.

TUCKMAN, B. W. *Conducting Educational Research.* New York: Harcourt Brace Jovanovich, 1972.

TURABIAN, K. L. *A Manual for Writers of Term Papers, Theses, and Dissertations.* (3rd ed.) Chicago: University of Chicago Press, 1970.

UNIVERSITY OF GEORGIA. "Policy on Human Research." Athens: University of Georgia, 1975. (Mimeographed.)

VAN DALEN, D. B. *Understanding Educational Research: An Introduction.* (2nd ed.) New York: McGraw-Hill, 1973.

VERNER, C. "Research-Based Publications." *Adult Education,* 1956, *6,* 226–233.

VERNER, C. "Definitions of Terms." In G. E. Jensen, A. A. Liveright, and W. Hallenbeck (Eds.), *Adult Education: Outlines of the Emerging Field of University Study.* Chicago: Adult Education Association of the U.S.A., 1964.

WEINBERG, S. "What to Tell America: The Writers' Quarrel in the Office of War Information." *Journal of American History,* 1968, *55,* 73–89.

WERTHEIMER, M. *Productive Thinking.* New York: Harper & Row, 1945.

WHARTON, C., JR. "The Green Revolution: Cornucopia or Pandora's Box?" In G. Ranis (Ed.), *The United States and the Developing Economics.* New York: Norton, 1972.

WHIPPLE, J. B. "University Training for Adult Educators. *Adult Education,* 1958, *8,* 93–97.

WHYTE, W. F. *Street Corner Society.* Chicago: University of Chicago Press, 1941.

Index

187494

154

Objectivity, issue of, 110–112
Operational definition, 92

Path analysis, method of, 135
PEARSON, E., 10
PEARSON, K., 10
PENNINGTON, F., 29
PETERS, J. M., 93
PETERSON, R., 8
PHILLIPS, B. S., 33, 84, 89, 92, 97, 98
PIAGET, J., 66, 116
POPPER, K., 103, 111
PREISS, J., 33, 65
Propositions, role of, 79–81

RAPAPORT, D., 116
Reliability, issue of, 106–110
Research: bibliographies on, 14;
  characteristics of, 7–11; computer
  search for, 31–32; continuing
  process of, 40; defined, 3–7; dependence on other disciplines by,
  18–19; descriptive, 16; descriptive-
  correlational-experimental loop in,
  134–135; design selection for, 33–
  35; development of, 14–21; field,
  63–77; future of, 127–128, 132–
  137; and graduate education, 12–
  13, 22–40, 119–128; incentives for,
  1–3; issues in, 100–118; literature
  on, 11–14; literature review for,
  31–33; methodological difficulties
  of, 106–118; perspectives on, 1–21;
  planning and practicing, 22–40;
  problem in, 27–31; proposal preparation for, 35–38; structural elements of, 27–35; theoretical frameworks of, 101–106; theory related
  to, 24; transition in methods of,
  16–18. *See also* Experimental research; Grounded-theory research;
  Historical research; Survey research
RHYNE, D. C., 93
RIVERA, R. J., 5–6, 8–9, 52
ROSENBERG, M., 33, 60, 61
ROYCE, J. R., 20
RUDDOCK, R., 126–127
RUSNELL, D., 20–21, 51, 53, 94, 130

Sampling, 36–37, 58, 70–71
SCHATZMAN, L., 33, 65, 70
SCHROEDER, W. L., 3, 4, 138

Scientific method, 5–7, 100–118
SELLTIZ, C., 33, 58, 107, 116
SHAH, F. B., 93
SHERWOOD, M., 111
SHILLACE, R., 20
SIEBER, S. D., 75
SIMMONS, J. L., 33, 65
SPENCE, R. B., 3, 13, 14
Stability, issue of, 106, 107–108
STANLEY, J. C., 33, 60, 78, 87, 88,
  90, 107
STEPHENSON, W., 116
STOGDILL, R., 111
STRAUSS, A. L., 33, 63–64, 65, 66, 69,
  70–71, 72, 73, 74, 76
STROUP, H., 52
STRUNK, W., JR., 40, 49
Survey research: analysis of, 50–62;
  data-collection instrument for, 58–
  59; descriptive and analytic types
  of, 52; design elements of, 55–61;
  and experimental research, 89;
  final steps for, 59–61; and
  grounded-theory research, 75–77;
  history of, 50–51; hypotheses for,
  56–57; nature and purpose of, 52–
  53; need for, 51–52; population
  and sample for, 57–58; problem
  defining in, 55–56; problems of,
  61–62; and triangulation of
  methodologies, 62
Syllogisms, 79–81

TAYLOR, A. J. P., 46, 150
Theory, 24, 66–67
THIEDE, W. B., 13
THORNDIKE, E. L., 6
THORNDIKE, R. L., 116
THORSON, J. A., 124
TOUGH, A., 9, 36
TRAVERS, R. M. W., 116
TROW, M., 61
TUCKMAN, B. W., 30, 33, 88
TURABIAN, K. L., 40

Validity, 9–11, 87, 106–110, 114–
  116
VAN DALEN, D. B., 28, 30, 80
VERNER, C., 3, 4, 9, 14, 24

WEINBERG, S., 46
WHIPPLE, J. B., 12, 19
WHITE, E. B., 40, 49
WHYTE, W. F., 64